FISHING
WITH
DAD

BY

DAVID LAMPTON MCKINSEY

© 1993, 2003 by David L. McKinsey. All rights reserved.

No part of this book may be reproduced, stored in a retrieval system, or transmitted by any means, electronic, mechanical, photocopying, recording, or otherwise, without written permission from the author.

ISBN: 1-4107-0583-8 (E-book)
ISBN: 1-4107-0584-6 (Paperback)

This book is printed on acid free paper.

1stBooks – rev. 01/09/03

DEDICATION

**These stories are for
everyone who has ever fished the
lakes and streams in the
Missouri Ozarks and who learned the
art while "Fishing with Dad."**

especially

David, Joel, Matt and Tim

CONTENTS

I   - Preface vii
II   - Fishing With Dad ix
III   - Introduction xiii

1. - THE MOUNTAIN MAN 1
2. - FISHING WITH GRANDPA 7
3. - LEFT OAR! RIGHT OAR! 16
4. - THE SUMMER OF '36 24
5. - FIRST VENTURE 36
6. - ON DANIEL BOONE'S TRAIL 43
7. - PENNYROYAL 50
8. - THE OLD MAN 60
9. - ON GETTING LOST 64
10. - FISHING WITH MOM 70
11. - WET CAMP 82
12. - THE COPPERHEAD 90
13. - WHAT DID HE SAY? 96
14. - BAIL! BAIL! 103
15. - THE MAN WITH SILVER BULLETS 112
16. - TO BUILD A FIRE 121
17. - JUST PASSING THROUGH 128
18. - CITY FISHIN' 133

19.	- THE ROAD TO THOMASVILLE	146
20.	- FISHING ON ELEVEN POINT	152
21.	- BIG SPRING	162
22.	- FISHING IN THE TREETOPS	169
23.	- FISHING WITH JERRY	176
24.	- THE OLD TACKLE BOX	186
25.	- THE LAST TRAIL	198
26.	- HARD LUCK JOE	210
27.	- SHOOTOUT AT PUTAH CREEK	219
28.	- GONE FISHIN'	229
29.	- FISHING WITH A LICENSE	242
30.	- THE FLOAT TRIP	257
31.	- LAKE LODGE	270
32.	- THE GREAT BLUE CAT	277
33.	- EASY FISHIN'	288
34.	- DAD'S BENEDICTION	298

PREFACE

If you're a fisherman, you're going to love this book. You may have had experiences similar to mine and you may know the exact locations where these stories took place. Even if you're not a fisherman, I think you'll find this book amusing and thought-provoking because it's more than just a collection of fish stories. It's also a story about people.

Every dad, mom, sister and brother has stories about their lives together that would give insight to others about their own lives. And every family has its patriarch who has stories to tell but who doesn't usually write them down. I have written these down because I think it's important that the events be passed along and the people not forgotten. Grandfather said, "will you carry on the record?" I hope that is what I have done.

Most of the people I should thank for helping me write this book are gone now. So if I made mistakes, exaggerated a little or just plain made it up, nobody can complain in the usual way.

Maybe at night when the moon is full and the night birds sing they'll come around and haunt me but I would like that.

David McKinsey

Novato, California

"Fishing With Dad"

You may talk about your pleasures
Of the Euchre club or ball,
Of the click of ruddy glasses,
Or the brilliant billiard hall,
Of the race course with its flurry
Or the opera's thrillin' sight,
That perhaps will speed the hours
Of a long or dreary night,
But to me the sweetest pleasure
That my soul has ever had,
Was when I was a fishin',
Was a fishin' with my Dad.

When the snow has left the hillside,
An' the sun's warm rays at last
Call the flowers from their slumber,
Sayin' that the winter's past,
When the drowsy life is humming,
An' the Whip-poor-will is heard,
An' the woodland seems enchanted,
By the song of many a bird,
Then dad sets my heart to thumpin',
As he says to me, "My Lad,
Don't you want to go a fishin',
Go a fishin' with your dad?"

Soon we're off to where the river
Like a mad or frightened steed,
Dashes o'er the rocks or Mill-dam.
(It is here the fishes feed.)
An' our expectations heighten,
As we cast our choicest flies
In the limpid gurgling waters
That conceal the wary prize,
An' we knew we'd surely catch some,
For good luck we always had
When we used to go a fishin',
Go a fishin' me and dad.

Daddy seemed to know the places
Where the big ones always stayed,
Back behind the rushin' waters
Of the Mill-dam, in the shade.
So with temptin' bait he'd manage
By the skill that he had gained,
To secure the largest fishes
That the fishin' place contained.
So when the summer time was comin',
I was always gay and glad,
For I'd get to go a fishin',
Go a fishin' with my dad.

What cared we for all the trials
That we'd meet ere we came back,
For the scorching of the sunbeams
Or mosquito's bold attack?
Could they check our jealous ardor,
Or dislodge us from our place?
For the pleasures of the fishin'
We could all such troubles face.
And tho many pests surround us,
Still what glorious fun we had,
When we used to go a fishin',
Go a fishin' me and dad.

Poor old daddy, may God bless him,
's gettin' rather aged now,
Snows of almost sixty winters
Rest upon his dear old brow,
And the sounding of his footsteps
Once so fearless, strong and bold,
Seems now to be gettin' feeble
Since my daddy's growin' old.
An' methinks the time's not distant,
(An' it makes my heart feel sad),
When no more I'll go a fishin',
Go a fishin' with my dad.

For old Time that never ceases
In his onward march of years,
Rests alike on me an' daddy,
An' it melts my eyes to tears
When I think the time is nearin',
For the years fly swiftly by,
When the boatman 'cross the river
Shall take daddy home on high.
But while God shall in his mercy
Spare the daddy an' the lad,
I shall live to go a fishin',
Go a fishin' with my dad.

June, 1902 Jno L. McKinsey

INTRODUCTION

Part of the fun of writing about the past is trying to explain how places and people have changed, whether for better or worse, and how yesterday fits in with today.

When I first fished the lakes and streams of the Missouri Ozarks in the 1930's, things were somewhat different. The perceptions might depend on your age. Older folks spend a lot of time adapting to change and trying not to notice it. Younger persons, faced with the historical evidence of their own past, are quick to say, "Boy, things have really changed since the old days!" So as you read these stories about "Fishing With Dad", which occurred in different time periods from the early 1900's to the 1990's, remember that "times change."

For instance today it's easy to plan a week-end at the Lake of the Ozarks. You just jump in your car, zip onto the Interstate and whiz down the four-lane to Osage Beach. But that was hard to do in the 1930's.

The state's main roads, U.S. 40, 50 and 66, were just two lane highways with a speed limit of 40 to 50 MPH. Many of the back roads that are paved today were then just graded trails or oiled earth. The good thing is that the old roads are still there and most of them have been vastly improved. But while you're whizzing along the 4 lane or on the cut-off, passing all those trucks, try to imagine what it was like for us, trapped in time as well as traffic.

In the 30's, the state and national park systems were just getting organized. Many of the attractions now visited by millions were still primitive. At Big Spring, for instance, the roads were just muddy trails. Today Big Spring is well-paved, offering all of the facilities of every National Park.

Montauk was chopped out of the wilderness by the C.C.C. and the State Park system was just getting it ready for public use. Alley Springs, with its bright red mill house, was at the end of a graveled road. Only a twisting trail went beyond it. The road to Eminence on the Jack's Fork was paved but beyond the bridge it was gravel all the way to Round Spring.

At this writing there still isn't a road to Greer Springs. Greer is wild, cold and dangerous. It's located a mile down the side of a steep timbered hillside, at the end of a narrow, unimproved, rock-strewn path. Recently the Government threatened to civilize the trail to Greer Springs but most Ozarkers have been against it. The Lake of the Ozarks started filling when Bagnell Dam was finished in 1931 but even as late as 1936 there were virtually thousands of miles of shoreline still undiscovered and unoccupied. Hundreds of resorts, marinas and attractions had not yet been built. Those that were operating then in places like Gravois Mills, Osage Beach or on the Gasconade have either disappeared or become something else.

It is hard to find some of the places and landmarks that I knew when I was "Fishing With Dad." Whenever I go back to Missouri I still search to find the shadows of old docks and fishing cabins. The thing to remember when looking for old locations is that everything is still there. It has just been overlaid by something else.

In the 1930's gas was cheap and tires were made out of real rubber. But an 8 cylinder Packard only got 9 miles to the gallon and those real rubber tires only lasted for about ten thousand miles if they didn't blow out first. One could expect to stop at "filling stations" more frequently than today, not only for gas but also for oil, radiator water, free road maps and refreshments.

Filling stations were more sociable than they are today. The boys who worked at the stations were locals and they liked to talk about their town. The man who owned the station could probably fix any machine ever built. The average stop took at least 20 minutes which was plenty of time to drink a Nehi soda, visit the outhouse or hear a new joke. Even the improved highways were never more than two lanes wide with only a graded shoulder. The U.S. and State highway departments were kept busy marking their highways with "passing" and "no passing" zones, speed limits, curve, hill and dip signs and even flood zone warnings.

All of the signs along the roads weren't put there by the highway department. The day of the roadside billboard was coming fast. Farmers rented the sides of their barns for hand-painted signs like "VISIT MERIMAC CAVERNS" and "BULL DURHAM" with an anatomically correct bull. The Burma Shave company put up multiple signs that told stories and sold their product. One series of five signs said, "HE MADE A PASS...WITHOUT LOOKING...NOW HE'S DOING...HIS OWN COOKING. BURMA SHAVE." The space between signs was based on an average speed of 45 MPH. Burma Shave signs were so fascinating that we watched for them and read them aloud as we passed. "A SCRATCHY FACE...WILL NEVER DO...UNLESS THE BRIDE...IS BEARDED TOO. BURMA SHAVE." I don't think there's a trace of those old signs today. They contributed to our education and amusement as dad drove the twisty-turny two lane roads of the Missouri Ozarks.

When I was growing up things were really a lot more complicated than they are today. Everybody talks about how "the old days" were "simpler times" but that's pretty much hogwash. Going fishing or camping took twice as much equipment as it does today. It took us 12 hours to drive from K.C. to St. Louis. Today you can drive it in five hours or fly it in 30 minutes.

But one thing that is a lot more complicated today than it was in 1938 is the radio. Wherever we lived in central Missouri in the 30's, the only radio stations we could get were powerful network stations in Kansas City and St. Louis - like WDAF and KMOX. There were very few local radio stations operating in Missouri towns except in Kansas City, St. Louis, St. Joseph, Jeff City and maybe Columbia.

It was the day of network radio. We tuned in for magical programs that sent our imaginations soaring. There was "Jack Armstrong", "Little Orphan Annie", "Jimmie Allen" and "Terry and the Pirates." Those were afternoon kid's shows. In the evening, after the six P.M. news, the whole country listened to "Amos & Andy", "Jack Benny" and "Fred Allen." It never occurred to any of us that towns like Rolla, Boonville, Lebanon or Osage Beach would ever have radio stations. What would be the point? In the 1930's you couldn't just drive down the road and pop into a warm and comfortable motel. It was a primitive time on the roads when there was nothing but "tourist courts" and they were few and far between.

A tourist court was a collection of small unimproved cabins clustered around a central office. In recreational areas the cabins were sometimes picturesque, made of logs with native stone chimneys, hidden in the trees close to a lake. On the main highways they were sometimes built next to a restaurant or a camp ground. There were hardly any tourist courts close to cities or big towns. If you wanted to stay overnight in Columbia, Jeff City or Joplin you stayed downtown in a hotel.

Today you can collect hundreds of brochures about wonderful places to stay and play around the Lake of the Ozarks. Little towns that were isolated on primitive roads and whose names have been forgotten are now part of the great rustic sprawl that goes all the way from Bagnell to Camdenton.

Down in the woods on the new Lake of the Ozarks in 1935 there were few tourist courts, some fishing camps, but no resorts and no hotels. The lake was still a primitive place. You had to bait your own hook.

Even before the lake was full entrepreneurs were putting up fishing camps that were little more than tourist courts with boat docks attached. Some of those early fishing camps became glamorous resorts. From Horseshoe Bend to Osage Beach resorts were built on the bones of old fishing camps. Of course you can't really fish at most of those resorts anymore but the dining and the views are great!

Other camps were built by fisherman who only cared about how many bass you caught that day. They tried to keep their camps simple and practical. The fanciest thing in camp might be a scaling platform with a fresh water pump. Most of these genuine fishing camps had to move from the burgeoning tourist areas. These days fishing is the last thing most tourists want to do.

Today a lot of people are excited about the big stars and bright lights of Branson, Silver Dollar City and Table Rock Lake. To me the exploitation of the Branson area is a sad story. Once Branson was a quiet little Shepherd Of The Hills town on the shores of Lake Taneycomo. Taneycomo was an experiment. They dammed up White River in 1912 to form the 14 mile long lake and to make electricity. Taneycomo was a small, picturesque lake whose shores were lined with fishing camps and resorts.

Rockaway Beach, where my Grandfather once owned property, was hidden away at the east end of the lake. The original Long Beach was located on Lake Taneycomo. Today it's hard to tell where the lake was since another dam down below formed Table Rock lake. The entire area is now one big lake and Branson, once an innocent little ozark town, is "Nashville West" with bright lights, big stars and very few echoes of yesterday. One of those echoes is the old main street of Branson, still as it was, and a little magazine called, "The Ozarks Mountaineer," which recalls the traditions and legends of the ozarks.

Back in the 30's there were no "fast food" drive-ins. But the roots of such food systems originated in the Ozarks. There were country restaurants in every town and some resorts provided dining rooms with genuine ozark fare. There was a fried chicken place on the road to Arrow Rock that featured "chicken in the rough." Southern fried chicken and french fries were served in individual baskets and everyone ate with their fingers. This was considered inovative at the time! It wasn't far from chicken in a basket to chicken in a bag to go. Guess who made millions with that idea!

In the old days every small town in Missouri had its square and the stores around it stocked everything the community needed. Shopping centers and suburbs hadn't been invented yet. And the idea that you would live in Fayette or Glasgow and work in Columbia or Jeff City would have sounded ridiculous to us. It took an hour and a half to get to Columbia from Fayette and what would you want to commute there for anyhow? I might add that this concept is still slow to catch on in central Missouri where many small towns still shop at the stores around the square.

Although many of the stories in "Fishing With Dad" took place the 1930's and '40's, there are some from much older times, like 1900 and 1902 when my Grandfather and his father went fishing and camping. There were no paved roads in Missouri then and some roads were nothing but trails. In those days people did serious traveling on trains and river boats. Horses, wagons and buggies bounced down primitive back roads connecting self-sufficient ozark communities. No man-made lakes drowned the deep wooded valleys of the Osage or the White rivers. Fishing trips were wilderness expeditions that required survival equipment and advanced woodsman skills. Trips like that sometimes lasted for weeks.

Having said all of that, I guess we're about ready to go fishin'! There's only one more thing for you to get straight. And that's the old lie that fish stories are always exaggerated or just plain untrue. Nonsense! Let me assure you that this claim does not apply to the stories you are about to read; every one of them is flat out true! After all, would Grandpa' lie?

##########

CHAPTER ONE

THE MOUNTAIN MAN

Fishing with Dad was unnerving for a kid of six or seven. That's because my daddy was a "Mountain Man," born a hundred years too late. Survival in the forest was serious business for his ancestors, who had cleared the woods and fought off Indians and wild animals from Kentucky to Missouri. Somehow dad had inherited the desire to escape civilization that had motivated his forebears and he found himself trying to apply it to the modern world into which he had been born.

Unfortunately for dad, the days of mountain men were over when he arrived on Earth. But he still tried to escape civilization. The Ozarks were his mountains. The dirt and gravel roads were his trails. Stray dogs were his bears. Hill folks were his Indians and the wily bass was his beaver. He could do without electric lights and radios. He preferred living in cabins with oil lamps and kerosene stoves. And just as the mountain men loved their horses, Dad cared a great deal about his Model "T" Ford, for the same reason. Dad's Ford took him away down rocky roads and into the uncharted wilderness, just as earlier his people had forced their wagons down muddy paths into the green gloom of river bottoms looking for land. Later when civilization and technology had produced fast cars and smooth highways Dad used them both, but only as escapes to get back to his wilderness.

Despite these mountain man tendencies, Dad tried to live like a civilized person. As a senior at Westminster College in Fulton, Missouri, he wore white ducks and a green eye shade while playing a good game of tennis. He smiled a lot, told funny stories, learned to smoke and had the usual ideas about girls.

But what he really liked to do was put on his old High School R.O.T.C. uniform and go out into the field. He went camping and slept in the mud. He got rained on and bitten by bugs. He knew how to shoot and skin squirrels and rabbits and he didn't care what he ate. As far as I know, there was nothing that Dad would not eat, including snakes and grass hoppers.

There was one thing he was very sensitive about though, and that was being called, "uncivilized."

"Who's not civilized?" he would growl. It was a natural rejection of what he knew very well to be true. But Dad accepted the world as he found it and he did not fight civilization. He was just more comfortable sitting on a log than in an easy chair. Dad wore a suit with a tie that was always crooked when he taught Sociology at Missouri U., Central College and Southern Methodist. His students all adored him. He would tell them stories from morning till night. He was always clean-shaven and, even though men didn't use deodorants in those days, he never smelled bad.

Dad adhered to the norm because he knew it was expected of him, especially by our socially-sensitive mother. Dad's own mother was a very cultured concert singer and his father was a respected preacher. Dad's immediate family was talented and intellectual. He was related to Sam Clemens, another basically uncivilized person. The two cousins had a lot in common, except that Mark Twain was able to channel his energies into books that sold rather well. Lots of people are like those two, of course, but on most of them the veneer of civilization has grown so thick that they have no desire to look for their roots. Dad didn't know about his roots either but he was driven by something visceral to get back to the mud, the creek bank and the hills and away from people.

By the time Mom and Dad were married in '26, dad was already a full-fledged escapist. His first job out of college was just what he wanted. He was a high school teacher in a little Ozark town on the Eleven Point river. He fished every morning and every night. He waded in up to his armpits, sat on muddy banks and wore no shoes. Then I came along.

Mother didn't want her baby born in the wilderness. She pushed Dad and made him get degrees and become a respectable professor. So I grew up to be a city boy. Little did I know that my father was a mountain man who would never be at peace unless he was in some wilderness, fishing, hunting, shooting and surviving like his ancestors had. And little did I know that Dad expected me to learn, through inherited aptitudes or something, the arts of survival that he already knew. But I was an awkward student and an unnatural woodsman.

To be fair, I don't think that Dad ever thought of himself as a "mountain man" and he probably would deny what I have written here about him. But as life got heavier for him, he spent a lot more time trying to escape.

One of Dad's greatest escapes would have been impossible a hundred years ago. He liked to get out on the highway in his '29 Chevy or his '34 Essex and drive till he dropped, going nowhere. When someone would ask him where he had been, he could answer truthfully, "nowhere."

As his family grew he was able to give his aimless escapes a goal. He would take my brother Jerry and me to some remote fishing camp in the Ozarks and try to teach us to like mud, bugs and fish slime. Jerry, very young at the time, was a willing student. He had the natural aptitudes that Daddy had expected to find in me. But I was a poor student and a fastidious city boy. Daddy was disgusted but he tried not to show it. Unfortunately,

Jerry did not bloom as a woodsman either as long as I was around to get all of Dad's attention.

After I left home Dad refined his escapes into full-blown adventures. Without my influence Jerry revealed himself to be a mountain man, too! During his last years in high school he and Dad developed a conspiratorial relationship which included long trips from Dallas up into Oklahoma. Dad's only purpose was to drive and drive and get away! He drank a little while doing it.

"Don't tell mother and I'll let you drive," Dad would say.

Jerry must have found the experiences pleasant. He learned to smoke and drink and drive long distances without tiring. They usually landed somewhere east of Neosho, deep in the Ozarks on a creek bank straight from Daddy's childhood.

There, trapping minnows and sleeping on the rocky bank, Dad would start all over again trying to find the thread he had lost somewhere. Jerry, learning Ozark lore from the source, was a willing student. Neither Dad or Jerry ever suspected that they were mountain men.

########

CHAPTER TWO

FISHING WITH GRANDPA

I have often wondered where my Grandfather McKinsey (John L.) got his huge store of lore about camping and fishing. He could have learned it from his soldier father who was forced to camp out for four years during the Civil War. Or he could have read stories about that avid sportsman, Teddy Roosevelt, who popularized hunting and fishing at about the time Grandpa was coming of age.

For whatever reason my Grandpa, John L., was quite an outdoorsman. He knew all about survival in the wilderness and how to catch all manner of fish and wildlife.

He knew about pitching wall tents, dry camps, minnow traps, fly fishing, hip boots and bass holes. He knew something else, too. He had discovered that going fishing was a good way to escape the grim realities of the everyday world.

Although Grandpa talked a lot about fishing and I saw many pictures that proved his prowess as a fisherman, I personally had never seen him catch anything.

But then I was only 6 or 7 and Grandpa was already 60-something. I kept nagging him to take me fishing but he never would. I think Grandpa was concerned about my small size and lack of experience.

Then came a Sunday afternoon when it became apparent that it wasn't Grandpa who didn't want me to go fishing, it was Grandma! That day Grandma went off with some of her singing buddies and wasn't coming back till after dark.

Grandpa said to me, "Son, I think it's time you learned to catch a fish!" Although Grandpa said he was going to teach me to fish, I later realized that he was supposed to be baby-sitting. To do a little fishing on a beautiful day he had to sneak off and take me with him.

We got to Turkey Creek right outside of Joplin in Grandpa's '28 Hudson. The Hudson had velvet seats and pull-down shades in the back. It was not a fishing car. But Grandpa piled the fly rods, tackle box and minnow bucket in the back seat with no worries because Grandma was not coming along that day. Grandpa drove to what was probably one of his favorite spots. We piled out on the bank of the swift-running creek, which looked to me more like a river. Although Turkey Creek was shallow and gravel-bottomed it was wide and noisy. Swift water plunging over big rocks made white-water sounds.

Willows hung over the water and dropped leaves in the current.

Grandpa pulled on his hip boots, or "waders."

"What about me?" I asked.

"You don't need 'em," he said, pulling his white mustache down into his mouth. "Just take off your shoes and socks and roll up your pants." I wore short pants, anyway.

"But what if..." I started.

"Just stay in shallow water!" he ordered. Although Turkey Creek was shallow at this point there were deep holes in it that could only be fished by someone in waders. "Here", he said, handing me a short fly-rod with a bug on the end of its line. Later

I found that this short rod had been my father's when he was a little kid.

Grandpa didn't hold my hand as we splashed out into the creek. He wanted to see if I would fall down right away. As I stood my precarious ground in the fast, frigid water, Grandpa showed me the rudiments of fly casting. He told me to cast my bug upstream, "out there", watch it float down and twitch it a little as it went. Then I was to pull it in and cast again. He watched me do that once, then waded off by himself.

I felt, right away, that this was futile. I would never catch anything and neither would Grandpa. Daddy had always fished from a boat, in deep water, or moving up and down a brushy shoreline. I knew that no one could catch anything this way. But I kept casting.

I don't know if Grandfather expected me to stay in one place or not, but he was moving, so I decided that I would too.

I moved down-stream, though I knew the water got deeper there. I went out further into the stream. It was quite wide and shallow. I supposed a fish would barely have enough water to cover its back as it swept down the stream looking for my bug.

Instead of catching a fish, my foot encountered a slick rock and in a second I was more a part of the river than before. "Blub!", and I went under.

"Hi-yuh!" Grandpa yelled, leaping toward me in great splashes. Though startled, I was all right. He grabbed my pole, which was floating away, pulled me up and looked at me. One of his hands still held his fly rod.

"Better stay put now, son," he told me. "See that shallow spot? Go over there."

"But the fish won't see my bug," I said.

"If you don't be careful, you'll be fish bait yourself!" he said, and squished off back to his hole, pulling his hat down. He waded in almost to his arm pits and began casting deep water.

"Sure," I thought, "he'll probably catch something and I won't." I had no sooner thought that, when a minor explosion took place at the end of my line. Something had smashed at my bug. "Pow! He tuk it!"

But I didn't know that. I just knew that something was trying to grab my pole out of my hands and it almost had it. "Grandpa!" I yelled, and back he came, flailing water, setting up a bow wave as he strode toward me.

His mouth was moving, but he was not cursing! Grandfather was a preacher and he never cursed!

"Dag-nab-it boy!" he said. "Dad-gummit! Dad-blame the dad-gummed thing!" Of course, that is not "cursing", although close to it.

"Dad-gummit!" I yelled back, trying to hold onto my pole. He took my rod and yanked at it long enough to see that it was not hooked to anything but a rock. Whatever had hit my bug had spat it out again and by this time it was no doubt in the deep pool where Grandfather's line would have been if he were not helping me. He looked forlornly toward that spot. I think the fish even jumped down there.

Meanwhile, I was hung-up. No amount of yanking would free the bug. "Dad-gummit!" I yelled again. "Quiet, boy,!" Grandpa growled. "Stay there," he said and slowly walked out to where the bug lay with its hook dug into a yellow rock. He pulled the bug lose and sloshed his way back to me. He handed me my pole and looked at me. Now he knew that if I caught a fish, I couldn't land it. And if I didn't catch one I would either get hung-up on a rock or slip and float off down-stream.

But one of Grandfather's best traits was his even temper. He loved to fish and to do so he would put up with a lot from me. He dismissed the idea of tying a rope to me and went back to his hole. I was left in the shallows with wet pants.

Nothing happened for maybe fifteen minutes. I was totally bored. Nothing was biting and I wasn't allowed to move and explore new spots.

Grandfather had not moved either and he was catching nothing. I began experimenting with my lure. It floated, but when I pulled on it, it "popped" and splashed water. This was supposed to convince a fish that the bug was helpless and fish love to attack anything that is helpless.

The bug made lovely bubbling and popping sounds when it was yanked back properly. Obviously, no fish was going to snap at the bug, no matter what.

So suddenly I gave the bug an extra-loud pop and drew back on the rod as if I had a fish. I guess I just wanted to see how it felt to imagine that I had a fish. I had forgotten all about Grandpa but when he heard the noise his head swung around and he started into action again. "Wait! Wait!" I yelled, "He got away!"

I pulled on the rod and started to reel in. Then I slipped again and sat back down in the water. I noticed Grandpa was also reeling in his line. He scooped me up and I thought I detected a deep rumbling in his chest. Grandpa was laughing!

"I guess you're the biggest thing I'll catch today," he said, and strode with me under one arm and his tackle under the other. When we got to the shore both of us were thoroughly soaked.

"Grandma's not going to like this," he said.

"But we can tell her it was a big fish that pulled you in, and I guess the Lord won't mind a little joke like that." Then he looked up to the heavens and seemed to have a thought. "Or were you trying to teach me a lesson out there, Lord?"

And the lesson was, I guess, that fishing is like praying. You can't do either one without concentrating.

########

CHAPTER THREE

LEFT OAR! RIGHT OAR!

When I was a kid one of the hardest things I had to learn was how to row the boat for Dad.

I always felt like I was with Washington crossing the Delaware and when the General would say, "Quiet, men!" my oar would splash and squeak, alerting all the Hessians. The finese of rowing a boat escaped me.

Of course Dad was very experienced at that sort of thing. Ever since Bagnell Dam filled the Lake of the Ozarks in 1931 he had fished all over the lake from the Grand Glaze to Warsaw. And he traversed it all in a 14-foot rowboat, sometimes with a 5-horse motor. Remarkably, Dad never owned a boat.

I never knew till I grew up how widespread his various fishing holes were. Some were 60 miles apart. When I was a kid they all looked alike to me. The lake was pretty deep, from 60 to 100 feet in the wide reaches. The water was gun-metal grey, always with a slight chop. Because of its hundreds of tributaries and the deep, sunken current of the old Osage River, the Lake of the Ozarks was never clear. The shores were wooded or were lined with steep, ancient, limestone bluffs. There were thousands of coves and inlets. Dad tried to fish them all, always in a rented boat and sometimes with me along.

Deep down Daddy was a hillbilly. He liked to go barefooted and sit in the mud. His grand-daddy had taught him how to run a trot line and how to fish with a cane pole.

But his father, the Reverend John L., was the first in our family to earn a living with his wits instead of by working the land. Reverend John L. was city folk. He was always on the cutting edge of technology. His was one of the first houses in Joplin to be wired for electricity. He owned a camera and took hundreds of pictures. And he caught bass with a casting rod and reel. Grandpa taught our Dad city fishing ways, using artificial lures and hand-tied flies. Dad might have thought he preferred a cane pole or a trot line, but when he saw his Dad catching big fish using bass plugs, he was hooked. Grandpa taught Dad how to stream-fish, wear waders and to use a fly rod. He taught him how to cast from a boat and how to maneuver that boat to just the right spot for a perfect cast. He learned what lures to use and how to row with the expertise of a Viking. He could bring a 14-foot wooden boat alongside a brushy or rocky bank and cast ahead to where the roots of a sunken tree or the tops of big rocks poked above the water. If he could get his lure to just the right spot, in-between two roots or at the base of a rock, he would often get a strike.

But whether there was a strike or not, it was the perfect cast that mattered. Dad took more satisfaction in getting his lure to the right place than in catching the fish that was supposed to be there.

Dad was a master at controlling a row boat and making the perfect cast. So when I came along, he tried to teach me the same skills. Little did he know that I would be so hard to train.

When Dad was teaching me to fish he did all the rowing for me. I admired his skill and the first thing I learned to do was to make the perfect cast. Sometimes I caught fish but most of the time I didn't.

All of that was well and good as long as my "guide" was rowing for me. But pretty soon, I realized that Dad wanted to fish, too. As soon as I learned to cast well, Dad told me to change ends with him so that I could row and he could fish.

I sat in the control center. I hefted the oars. They swung easily in their locks. I looked behind me. That was where we were supposed to go.

"O.K., kid, remember when you pull the right oar, the boat goes left. The left oar brings the boat right. Got it?" This was practically the extent of his teaching. "Both oars is full speed ahead. Push on the oars for a full stop. Push on one oar and pull on the other for a speed turn. Got that?"

"Uh..."I said, noncommittally.

"O.K., let's go!" I manned the oars, dipped them in the water and pulled. A mighty splash from the left oar sent the bow right. I had not intended that. I pulled the right oar to bring us back on course, and pulled deep with both oars.

"I want to fish that point," Dad said, pointing over my shoulder, "then into the cove and back around all the brush in the shallow end, then back up the other side. Let's go, both oars!"

Rowing is hard work. It's not so bad when going flat out in deep water, but later I discovered that I was expected to navigate like Nelson at Trafalgar.

"O.K., even her out and let me get a crack at that stump," Dad would say. That meant stop oars and push a little with the left. "Come on, get closer," Dad urged. I would pull mightily with both oars.

"Hold it!" Dad said softly. Stop oars. Here came the cast from the World Master. It was too far out. I could see Dad's pained look. So I pulled with both oars to get closer. "Wait a minute," Dad cried, "I'm trying to reel in!" Dad reeled frantically, making the top-water lure do things that no fish would believe.

"Let her go, now, we're coming in." I leaned on the oars. A slight current or something made the oars two tillers and the boat skewed to the left.

"Right oar!" Dad ordered. Right oar it was. The boat lost way and turned right but did not straighten out. "Left oar, for krissake!" Dad fumed. Dad had not explained to me about compensation. It was always just, "Left oar!" Then, "Right oar!" He probably thought that I would instinctively know how to compensate. But this detail must have been left out of my DNA. I had to learn by sad experience and of that I had plenty.

Although my rowing became at best only satisfactory, Dad did try to do a lot of fishing while I was at the oars. The situations would have been hilarious to anyone else, but for us it was torture. Dad could never quite reach the log, the rock, or the pool that he wanted. Or we would be too close and he would catch a tree. However, Dad would never directly criticize me for putting the boat in the wrong place. He treated my mistakes like some circumstance over which he had no control.

But he would vocalize: "Left oar! Right oar!"

As I have said, when Dad was rowing he always put the boat just where it should be. I studied his style, but I couldn't figure out how he did it.

I continued to botch things up. But the worst times were when Dad would actually catch a fish and had to rely on me to keep the boat straight so he could land it. "Bring her around," he would plead. "Get the oar out of the way! You've got my line! Oh, hell, he got off."

Then there was gloom and tension. My face was grim and my throat tight and I fought tears. There was nothing worse than Dad losing a fish because I had done something wrong. The only thing worse might have been once when I was back casting, my lure whizzed through the air in a low trajectory and hit Dad right in the head!

"O.K., kid," Dad said with remarkable patience, "let's get in there and try again." This particular time I was successful in wrenching our craft to the right spot and Dad actually caught another fish. This time he didn't say a word. With tongue between his teeth and a gleam in his eye, he landed a 3-pound bass. It hung, dripping and flipping over the boat.

Then Dad smiled and said, "Not bad, kid," as if he didn't really mind all my goofs.

But then, his face changed. "Back oars! We're going ashore!"

The overhanging branches were hitting the boat. I ducked, but Dad couldn't. The tree limbs just missed his head and scraped his body. With his hands in front of his face, he growled, "Get us out of here. The fishing is ruined now, anyway."

There are many tales about how I learned to row a boat for my Dad. The fact is, I could never row to suit him. But though he was pained, injured and frustrated, he never ridiculed me or brought it up with anyone else. When my performance improved, Dad actually complimented me. And when it came to rowing for myself later in life, everything he said and did miraculously came back to me. Today, I can put a rowboat just about anywhere.

Though Dad is gone now, I can still hear in my mind his big voice saying, "Left oar! Right oar! Come on, kid, let's go!"

########

CHAPTER FOUR

THE SUMMER OF '36

When I was 6 I thought the summer would never end. I actually forgot about time and I was shocked when Mother told me I had to go back to school.

At the age of 9, when I was more sophisticated, there was a summer that I just hoped would never end. It was 1936 and Dad was moving around a lot working with the Government's new Transient program. He had just been transferred from St. Joseph to a new camp down at the Lake of the Ozarks. We had lived in two different houses in St. Joseph and I had gone to two different schools to finish the 3rd grade.

It had not been a happy year for me. When school was finally out that spring I was really relieved. Mom and Dad were also happy because they had just been waiting for school to be out so they could move closer to Dad's work. I didn't know anything about their problems or what was happening. Kids usually just take things as they come. But what they were planning to do was to give Jerry and me a lifetime of direction and memories.

Through some arrangement I never understood, Mom and Dad were given the opportunity to spend the summer, three whole months, in a large cabin on the Lake of the Ozarks. The cabin, a yellow clapboard shotgun house, had once belonged to the governor of Missouri. The Governor had spent some time there when the lake was filling, probably for publicity purposes. It is barely possible that we got the cabin because Mom's uncle on her father's side had once been the governor. If that was so, it was one time when being a Stark had paid off.

That summer on the lake was the first real summer of the rest of our lives. It was the first time we had ever been to the new Lake of the Ozarks. The cabin was located on a short cove just south of the new Bagnell Dam. They called our little community of cabins, Lake Ozark. In the summer of '36 bread was 10 cents a loaf and eggs were 20 cents a dozen. Everything was cheap, but then Dad was only making $2,500 a year! So we still didn't have food to waste. For snacks we ate crackers and mustard. It was French's yellow mustard (9 cents). Nobody had ever heard of "Gray Poupon."

Since we were on the first settled arm of the lake, the cabins were all rather large. They were, or had been, summer houses for city folks. They all had docks, some with large cruisers in them. Lights were strung everywhere. At night the cabins were all lit up. Boats came in after dark flashing red and green running lights. On warm evenings, sounds carried across the lake. Cook pots clattered, screen doors slammed and the smell of kerosene wafted into the night air. Charcoal briquettes hadn't been invented yet. Happy voices shouted to one another. Echoes of radio shows floated across the bay. "It's the Jack Benny Show!" From one cabin came the sounds of a Victrola, playing records from a vaudeville show. "The Two Black Crows" told corny jokes that were somehow hilarious.

"How we gonna remember where we caught all those fish today?"

"We'll know because I marked the spot."

"How's that?"

"'Cause I put an "X" on the bottom of the boat!" The summer of '36 at Lake Ozark was an ideal time for Jerry and me. At the age of five, Jerry was not yet competitive. In fact he looked up to me then. I thought nothing of it, because it seemed to me to be the natural state of things. I thought that the relationship would never change. It was natural that big brothers looked after little brothers and little brothers admired their big brothers. Naturally, I showed Jerry how to do things and we were both pleased when Jerry caught on. It never occurred to me that Jerry would one day disagree with me or try to get the upper hand. That day would come only years later and of course to my complete surprise and consternation.

In the summer of '36 we were just two guys. I was the oldest, therefore I All little brothers should stay 5 years old.

I don't know exactly how Mom felt about that summer. The little yellow cabin down by the lake was a far cry from the fancy brick duplex we lived in in St Joseph. Mother was a natural aristocrat, although some would have called her a social climber. When Dad moved us into the brick duplex and bought her the Baby Grand, Mom kind of bloomed. She threw parties for the people Dad worked with. She had a natural gray streak in her hair and when she put on her long lavender velvet dress, she was a stunning beauty. One handsome fellow, tall and with a Clark Gable mustache, paid her particular attention. We were told that he was Uncle Bill. Years later I realized that "Uncle Bill" was an imposter.

Now, Mom was stuck down here in the woods wearing cotton dresses, her beautiful hair limp in the summer heat, far away from "Uncle Bill." I don't think that she was really unhappy though. She was wise enough to see that her role was not that of a ravishing beauty in a velvet dress mixing at cocktail parties with good-looking guys like "Uncle Bill."

In any case Mother didn't seem to mind living in the woods surrounded by country people as long as it was only for the summer. Mother was very supportive of Dad and her children but I'm sure she dreamed of moving back to a city, where she could have nice things around her, and maybe even wear the lavender velvet dress again. Incidentally, she made that dress herself.

Maybe Dad moved us down to the lake that summer to keep his attractive wife away from temptation. Maybe he moved us there so that his kids would have the benefit of learning about nature and the great outdoors. Or maybe he moved us to the lake because Dad felt that it was an ideal place to live, and not just for the summer.

I'm sure that it was Dad's secret dream to live in a cabin by the lake where he could fish every morning and night, wear old clothes and roll in the dirt when he felt like it.

To Dad, Lake Ozark was perfect. He could almost fish from his front door. He didn't have any grass to cut or house to keep up. He could drive up to the highway and be at work in half an hour.

Of course, Dad knew that he couldn't keep us there forever. He had to find us a house in a town big enough to provide a good school for Jerry and me. All of our furniture and stuff was in storage and he had to find a nice place to put it in that his wife would like. He probably sat around on warm summer nights smelling the water and listening to fish jump, wondering why he couldn't just stay there. He tried to get us on his side by teaching us all he could about fishing and camping.

"Do you like it here?" he would ask us.

"Uh huh, yeah, sure," we would say.

"Would you like to live here all the time?"

"Doesn't it get cold?" I asked in my literal way.

"Sure, but..."

"Mom says there's no heater. We'd freeze. Besides..."

"O.K., O.K! Let's get to bed," Dad would scowl. He knew all of this. It was a summer place. For Dad, it was only a dream.

The day-to-day routine of living at the lake that summer escapes me. The parts that I remember would probably take up only one day in real time.

It was early dawn on a quiet summer morning. I had put my tackle together the night before so all I had to do was stumble down the steps, grab my rod, go to the edge of the lake and start casting. It was still dark when I started.

I cast into the dark lake. I could hear the lure hit the water, then I reeled in till the plug hit the top of my pole. I kept doing this, hoping that something big would hit my lure.

Eventually, it got light enough for me to see. There was a mist on the lake's surface. It was quiet, calm, perfect for casting. Now that I could see I began to aim at certain spots. There was a big log out about 15 feet. I cast at it, but the plug went over the log and plopped on the other side. Now the plug floated unseen behind the log and I was afraid to yank it back and get hung up. Just as I was carefully pulling the lure up over the bark there was a tremendous explosion behind the log. I had a huge strike!

In fact, the fish had hit just as my lure was dangling from the log. I yanked back on the line but the fish had other ideas. He ran under the log and jumped, trying no doubt to tangle up my line. But he wasn't quite successful and I horsed him back behind the log and actually up and over before - he got off!

By this time Dad had heard all the wallowing and was out on the porch looking interested.

"It was a big bass!" I yelled. "He was behind the log but he got off when I went to pull him in."

"Oh?" was all Dad said.

"I had him! I had him! He was big, too!" I reeled in my line, experiencing for the first time the frustration of losing a big fish when no one was watching. It was bad enough to lose the bass, but even worse that no one would believe it. For a nine year old it was devastating. I put my rod away for that day.

Later in my composite day, actually probably a few weeks later, Jerry and I went swimming. Swimming in a lake on a natural beach was something city folks had a hard time doing.

City swimming pools had smooth concrete bottoms that you could see because the water is clear and clean. The only waves were caused by other swimmers.

Natural lake beaches had sandy and rocky bottoms, with weeds and sticks on them. The depth fell off unevenly and there were unexpected holes. The water was full of sediment and other natural ingredients, including fish. You couldn't see the bottom unless you went under water with your eyes open and got very close. Once you accepted all of that, the swimming was great.

Our beach had been cleared and was clean. A rope on floats marked the edge of the shallow water. "Shallow" was about 5 feet. Beyond the rope, who knew the depths that would swallow us? We tried to find out by kicking off from the float and out into the forbidden depths. It was always a thrill to put your foot down and find no bottom. Flailing and thrashing, we would scuttle around the surface like beetles, knowing that to keep breathing we had to kick (tread water) and thrash (swim). We were usually much too tense to last long in deep water and we would desperately lunge for the floats.

That afternoon we were just floating around in shallow water playing with a Dizzy Dean beach ball when we heard a "crack" and felt a tingling shock in the water. We looked up and saw a black cloud to the northwest bearing down on us. It was a typical Missouri thunder storm, full of lightning and heavy rain. As we watched, another slashing stroke of white lightning struck the water about five miles away. ZAP! We got it again. That did it. We leaped out of the water and ran to the cabin. Mom would probably not believe it. We ran up the steps, yelling, "We were shocked! We were shocked!" Mom opened the door with a questioning face. Just then the rain came sweeping over the lake like a curtain and began pounding the cabin.

"Where are your clothes, dear?" Mother said calmly.

It could have been a tornado and Mother would just look around like nothing was happening. We both spoke at once, screaming about getting shocked in the water, soaked in the rain, how our clothes were out there on the beach and would she please shut the door!

In another few minutes the storm had blown over and the sun was shining. We went back to get our soaked clothing, but we didn't go back in swimming that day!

Memories are like old desks and dark closets. When you start digging around, forgotten things come up and for a few moments the past seems to live. The trouble is, the past cannot live within the present without a penalty. Someone once asked, "Where does time come from?" The answer is, "From the future."

########

CHAPTER FIVE

FIRST VENTURE

This is another story by my father about "The Old Man." It is actually an account of the first fish I ever caught while I was "Fishing With Dad."

I was kneeling and holding the prow of the John boat that we both preferred for fishing. The old man was inching his way off of the dock, peering downward to see if his legs were in position for a safe landing in the boat. He maneuvered somewhat and finally was astride the plank that served as a seat. He appeared embarassed by his awkwardness.

"I felt plum foolish trying to get in this dadgummed boat," he said without rancor. "Hand me my gear and after that you'd best

be untying your end and fixin' to shove off. Fishin' time was some time ago."

While he was still giving instructions the boat was untied, the motor started and we were headed toward the spot the old man had previously picked. It was a log-strewn cove with overhanging branches of trees. The old man had a way of picking likely-looking spots.

He said he "thought like a fish" but it was really his experience as a fisherman that made him an expert.

"Sure is a perfect evening for fishing," was his comment and I nodded. The evening was perfect indeed. The lake had tiny waves from the slight breeze. The sky was cloudless. Schools of minnows were cruising near the surface promising feeding fish. To make it perfect, a fish jumped in the end of the cove where we were headed.

Sometimes the picture can belie reality, but no sooner had the old man placed his bass bug at the base of a stump than a bluegill tried it on for size. The lure was too big for the perch, but it was a good sign. His next try brought a splash and the old man timed his setting of the hook just right to bring on a brief but spirited tussle. Afterwards he held up a "keeper", I thought, but he threw it back with a muttered, "too small." By the time I had my outfit rigged he had another one on his line and this time when he held it up for inspection he kept it.

"I told you it was a perfect evening for fishing. Sort of reminds me of an evening spent with my oldest boy - let me see - that would have been in the late thirties when I was much younger." He stopped as if to relish the memory a bit longer.

"Oh, Oh," I thought, "Here comes, another yarn." But that instant a "good-un" snatched my bug and I was too busy to listen to half-remembered tales. The old man watched the struggle intently, then instructed me to bring the fish to his end of the boat for landing.

I told him I could handle it and I brought aboard a nice "skillet-sized" bass. "Throw it back", the old man snorted. "That's just bait."

"Yeah? Well, it's my bait so I'll just keep it." I put the bass on my stringer and ignored the old man's outburst. I thought I caught the word, "childlike" in his tirade, but I suspect that he was just regretting that he had let his own catch go. I expected more angry words but in a moment he blandly resumed his story.

"As I was saying, this whole evening serves to remind me. There's the dock, ripples on the water, this cove, that log there. Of course, it was some different. It was a small boy trying to step into a canoe properly instead of me and this ancient John boat. But mostly it was just the same except of course, I didn't have you along to argue with me about everything."

He scowled and I watched as he snaked his fly expertly under the overhanging branch of a tree and set his bug down at the end of a rotting log. His effort was rewarded by a veritable explosion as a bass went after his lure. He played with it for some time and then led the worn-out fish to my end of the boat. He looked at me suspiciously as I unhooked the nice sized fish.

"It's smaller than the one you threw back, so…"

"Don't you dare," he snorted and grabbed his fish. He stared at me for a moment, muttering something, then resumed his story.

"Well, sir, this boy's evening started off poorly. His first try landed on the bank and the next hung on a tree limb. When this happened I told the kid that squirrels don't go for those things. I would guess he felt a mite sheepish because he slumped down, turned and glared at me something fierce. After that, though, he got his former attitude and relaxed somewhat. The boy was middling good for a beginner.

"When we rounded the point and saw the cove I caught my breath. You never saw such a snaggle of brush, logs, tree limbs and such like. Why it would take an expert like me - or you," he added this last with a grin, "to flip a fly in there properly."

"But that was where the fish were, if any, and I kept the canoe in position for fishin' just as I would at any other bank. You can bet, though, that I had my fingers crossed waiting to see what the boy would do. The kid didn't say a word but I could see him eyeing that mess of brush sort of scared like.

"The kid made a couple of brave attempts but the fly fell way short of where it should have been and I kept the canoe headed for the far bank. I had spotted a log just off the bank and told him to aim his bug between the log and the bank. After considerable squirming he got up his courage and made a try. When the bug landed square on the log he was disgusted. But his disgust changed to horror when the bug fell off the log on the bank side and a bass tried to swaller it!"

"It was a time for prayer," I couldn't resist inserting, "and I suppose your prayers were answered promptly."

"It wasn't a praying time!" he retorted sharply and whipped his fly with unusual vigor. My remark had obviously shaken his usually good aim for he promptly got hung on a piece of brush.

"As I was saying before I was interupted - dang it, we'll have to go in there and get my bug - the boy sat there for an instant, then he horsed that bass clean over the log. I reckon it was reflex on his part but that was the best thing to do, though he didn't know it at the time and later he apologized for the action.

"After that, with a bit of coaching from me, he handled that bass like a veteran fisherman and got it in the canoe in good style. Right away he wanted to go home and show his mother the bass he had caught but I vetoed that. There was a good hour of fishin' time left.

"Although I was very pleased with my boy, my pride in him couldn't match his happiness. Boy, was he ever tickled! The bass wasn't as big as the one of yours I wanted to throw back, but it was a keeper that's for sure. So in line with my edict he half-heartedly fished some more but I could see his mind wasn't on it. So I handed him the paddle and told him to show me how good he was at handling the canoe while I finished fishing the rest of the cove. Right off I could see that he was out of his league paddling for a fisherman. It takes a great deal of know-how to do that, you know. Oh, I got in a couple of hurried casts but I realized then that the boy was headed for home and I didn't say anything."

The old man looked at me then and smiled. "By the way, there was another difference between that evening and this. Back then I didn't have you along to handle the boat for me."

He cleared his throat and looked away. Then he whipped his lure close to another log and came up with the biggest bass of the evening!

######

CHAPTER SIX

<u>ON DANIEL BOONE'S TRAIL</u>

If you had asked my Grandmother Stark about Daniel Boone, she would likely have said, "Oh, you mean Uncle Dan'l?" I got that stuff all the time when I was growing up. She and her Enloe forbearers said they were related to everyone from Abraham Lincoln to Kit Carson, including Daniel Boone. Boone did live in Missouri back in the 1820's, and I suppose that anything is possible. But telling me at the age of 10 that I was related to the great tracker, Indian fighter and bear-killer, Daniel Boone, did not boost my self-confidence as much as they had probably hoped.

It was mid-afternoon on a summer's day in the 1930's. We put the boat into the lake after coming out of the woods onto a rocky beach about a mile from camp. The camp was not a fishing lodge, but a U.S. Government Transient Camp which Dad had helped to build. Now, Dad was the ramrod there. He carried a pistol and a knife and he managed to get about 60 guys of various ages and conditions to do what he told them. It was probably the high point of his life. He was 35 at the time and I was 12.

There was a boat-launch site three miles away at the end of the peninsula, but to save time Dad liked to crash through the woods, carrying the boat and all his tackle down a dim trail. It was closer to the lake, but a lot more primitive than the dock. Dad had me to help him carry the boat, which was a fairly heavy wooden canoe with a square stern.

We shoved off and fished all afternoon and I remember catching at least two Smallmouth Bass. We also did some swimming from the boat. I tried not to think about how deep the water was there, about 30 feet I guess, but I never swam too far from the boat. Dad was more interested in teaching me how to get into a boat from deep water without overturning the boat.

After about three hours, we pulled the boat out, cleaned the fish and gathered things up for the trudge back through the woods. It was about 6 in the evening and I could smell cook-house smoke coming from back at the camp. At that time, we lived about 15 miles away at

Kaiser, population 50, but quite often Dad would stay at camp for dinner. At times he would have one or all of us along with him and sometimes we would spend the night there. It didn't occur to me then that the schedule was always varied. I assumed that Dad was the Big Dog at the camp and set his own hours. He did have a boss, but I didn't know it at the time. I knew that Dad was happy. He got whatever he asked for from his men and his staff. He didn't drink, he smoked a pipe and he seemed to be thoroughly in his element. It must have been his German side that liked this leader arrangement. His Scotch-Irish side endeared him to his men, to whom he would tell stories from morning till night.

Back at the beach, we started into the brush. We carried the boat and I saw very little, bouncing along in the back behind Dad. We encountered no snakes or anything else and soon we were back at the edge of the camp, where we put the boat down by a rack the men had built. It was then that Dad looked troubled and snapped his fingers!

"Damn, I left my knife on the beach!" He slapped his belt where the empty scabbard was. He had cleaned our fish on the beach and somehow he had forgotten the knife. Or, had he? "I'm sure!" he said.

"Well, I guess...no, hell I got to go to the mess hall for a meeting at 7. Kid?" he looked at me, "would you go back and get it?

"Well, sure," I said uncertainly. "I guess I can."

"What's the matter?" Dad said suspiciously. "You know where it is. Just go back and get the knife and meet me in the mess hall for dinner. Thanks, kid."

He turned away and I walked back to where the boat was.

So I was related to Daniel Boone, eh? Let's see, where was that trail? It had seemed plain enough when I was with Dad, but now it looked like impenetrable forest. There weren't even any broken sticks or bent twigs to indicate we had been there. I noticed a couple of Dad's men watching me, so I plunged in.

I was not at all sure that I was going in the right direction and it was getting dark. Dad had not given me the flashlight. He only had one! That one flashlight lasted for several years until one of us, probably me, dropped it overboard.

So I clawed my way to the beach and looked for Dad's knife in the failing light. I found where we had cleaned the fish but the knife wasn't there. I looked and looked with a sinking feeling. I would have to go all the way back through the woods in the dark and tell him that I hadn't found the knife! Daddy's efficient German side also had a mean streak and I did not want to face his wrath. I stayed longer than I should have trying to find that knife. Then I told myself we would have to find it later and I started back. I was tired and a little panicky now. It was dark! It had been dark in the woods all afternoon. Now it was black! Bending my head, I just pushed my way through the trees and bushes and didn't even bother looking for a "trail." I felt like a failure and I was scared besides.

When I finally broke through and out to the edge of camp, I was out of breath, scratched up and a little teary-eyed. Nobody was there, and I saw that the boat from where I had started was a hundred yards to my left! I had made my own trail through the woods!

So I dragged myself to the mess hall where Daddy and a few of his men were sitting around telling stories. Is that all they ever did, I thought, just tell stories to each other? Dad saw me and jumped up. I put my hands out and looked helpless. "The darn knife wasn't there," I said, miserably.

"Hey, kid," Dad said. "I'm sorry to put you through that, but I found my knife in the tackle box after you left."

"Great!" I shrieked. But I thought, he could have least whistled for me. He could have done a number of things to relieve my mind and body, but he didn't. I was ticked off! My Cherokee side was showing and I wanted his scalp!

"Did you get lost?" Dad asked.

"Hell, no! I growled.

"What's that?"

"Nothing. No, I was fine." I kicked a rock.

"Can I have a drink of water now? And what's for dinner?" I asked.

Dad grinned. "Your favorite," he said. "It's creamed chipped beef on toast. And here," he handed me the lost fishing knife, "use this to cut it with. It's yours now, anyway."

Well, that helped somewhat. I looked at him and took it without a word. It didn't bother me that the last thing the knife had been used for was to gut a bass. I did like the knife.

To this day, I don't know if Dad set up that lonely and scary thrash through the woods to test my courage and woodsmanship. And I never did admit to him that I was lost and scared. If it was a test, the fact that I got back was a passing grade. Dad's training worked in mysterious ways and I don't think he believed that I was related to Daniel Boone.

But I caught him looking at me as I wolfed down my beloved chipped beef and I thought I saw a self-satisfied smile on his face.

########

CHAPTER SEVEN

PENNYROYAL

Pennyroyal is a plant in the Mint family that grows in the Missouri Ozarks. It was used by the old-timers to keep "skeeters" away. When Pennyroyal is crushed, it exudes a pungent odor not unlike Citronella, but more spicy. When Dad and I went camping, we always tried to pitch our tent close to some Pennyroyal.

There were squalls over the Lake of the Ozarks that day, back in 1940. It was getting rain-dark as we pushed off in the old wooden boat with the 5-horse Johnson. This time there were three of us - Dad, Jerry and me, with a hundred pounds of gear. The equipment included a pup tent, pots, pans, canned beans, a carton of eggs, bacon, coffee, all of our rods and tackle and one flashlight.

Although flashlights were fairly common by 1940, Dad still had a World War One mentality about them. To Dad, flashlights were exotic. In his day only one was issued per company and it was carried by the Sergeant. When Dad told you to carry the flashlight, it was a big deal. I don't think Dad ever owned more than one flashlight!

Dad wrapped the rope around the Johnson and yanked it to life on the first pull. This was remarkable and kept him in good humor. Dad headed the overloaded boat toward a brushy island about half a mile from the Twin Bays Resort dock. The plan was to do some evening casting, then make camp and do some early dawn fishing around the island. But about half way over a thundersquall broke with heavy rain. I thought that should have killed the evening fishing. But instead of turning back to our nice, dry cabin with the battery operated radio, Dad stubbornly pushed on while we bailed the boat.

Camping on a deserted island covered with brush, rocks, bugs and other unpleasant inhabitants is bad enough on a good day. But this was a wet, windy day quickly turning to night and it struck me as an idiotic time to camp-out. Yet I didn't dare grumble because we were men!

Dad cut the motor at just the right moment and the sluggish old boat crunched ashore. I was bowman, so I leaped ashore with the tie rope and pulled the boat further up on the rocks. Then the unpacking began. Even though the thunderstorm had rumbled on past, the sky was still overcast and spitting rain. Dad seemed fatalistic as we set up camp. He looked like he was thinking, "Who cares if it's raining? We're camping and away from home, Mother and civilization."

I always thought that Dad had other motives besides just fishing to get out in the woods with his boys. He was always trying to "make men out of us." Perhaps this wet camp was just another way for us to prove that we weren't "sissies."

It stopped raining and the stars came out. That helped a little bit, but finding dry wood was impossible. Dad set up a rock fireplace and coaxed a lot of brush to burn in it. Jerry stripped the bark from some logs I had brought and soon they were reluctantly smouldering. They made enough heat to cook supper. Dad called it "a fisherman's supper": eggs, bacon and beans, but no fish. It was good, but there was no place to sit because everything was wet.

As we stood around sucking up beans I wished we were back in our cabin. But I don't think Dad wished that at all because he always seemed happy in adverse circumstances. I guess that was part of the training. It never took with me. I stay in dry cabins whenever I can and I keep six flashlights handy at all times!

In situations like that wet night on the island, my budding character tended to reveal flaws. I'm sure Dad thought he could mend those flaws by dumping me in a bad spot and making me work my way out. It might have succeeded except that I knew that if Dad and Jerry were there, they would do all the work! I wasn't really lazy, though. I was just not the pioneer type. On this wet, moonless night all of my flaws were showing, but I was not totally useless. I carried things. I got the firewood but Dad built the fire. Jerry watched Dad closely but I appeared to be uninterested and stood around with my hands in my pockets.

Dad, though a professional teacher, was reluctant to teach us how to build a fire or cook. He thought that we should somehow just naturally know such things. Although Jerry was a good observer and I took orders well, neither of us asked any questions for fear of seeming to be dumb.

So we each had our roles. Dad was the leader. He navigated, picked spots, took care of our tackle and did all the cooking. Jerry seemed to be a natural-born woodsman. He pitched tents, hung utility lines, tied knots and always seemed to be "at one" with nature. I never did find out where Jerry learned all that. He knew, by eye, the right place to pitch a tent. He might rely on me to hold up the tent while he inserted the poles, but that's all I did while he pounded pegs and otherwise set up camp. Jerry also knew how to blaze trees, cut up vegetables for stew, hang food bags away from racoons and otherwise survive in the wilderness. He and Dad even looked like woodsmen, with their dirty pants, shirts covered with burrs, hats smudged with ashes and mud. I was just the opposite. I stood around and tried to keep clean while they rolled in the mud and scratched their backs on trees like bears.

Although we both had the same genes, Jerry's seemed to contain more DNA from those fishing and camping fools, Grandpa John L. and Great-Grandpa Granville. My genes seemed to favor our other Grandpa, Della Lemuel Stark, a civilized lover of creature comforts.

Thus in my role as a watcher and carrier, I was sent to fetch the Pennyroyal. As soon as supper was over and the dishes washed with sand from the beach, Jerry holed-up in the tent and went to sleep.

Daddy, as was his custom, sat close to the smouldering campfire, smoking and gazing blankly out at the dark spot where the lake was. Who knows what he was thinking? I would not sit around the fire because there was nothing to rest on or lean against except sharp rocks and wet trees. Today when I go into the woods the first thing I pack is a chair! Dad and Jerry preferred squatting. Maybe it was the Indian blood that made squatting easy for Jerry. I had Indian blood in me too and I had certain skills that must have been helped by this heritage. I was good at fishing. I could whang a knife at a door and make it stick. I could shoot the eyes out of a snake. I even liked snakes! Fish blood and guts didn't bother me. I had a natural sense of direction and I could "tell" the weather. But I just couldn't stand to be a slob.

I thought about this as Daddy blew his nose with his fingers and looked absurdedly happy squatting on his rock by the fire. You would never know he was a college professor.

"Going to bed, kid?" he asked. I told him, yeah, but not until I got a bunch of Pennyroyal to keep the bugs away. I hated bugs. Daddy loved bugs. He wouldn't even kill one unless it threatened him.

"O.K., bring me some, too," he said. Since there was only one pup-tent, Daddy was sleeping on the ground. He had an army blanket on a canvas ground cover and a make-shift rain flap held up with sticks. Dad didn't like the rain flap because it obscured his view of the stars. But this night there was nothing to see in the sky except for clouds of approaching mosquitoes.

So I got an armload of Pennyroyal. I stuck two branches in the ground around Dad's rain flap. I took the rest to the tent, where I presumed Jerry was sleeping. I put a few pieces around our bedding and hung some from the tent ropes. The tent had no floor, of course, just a ground cloth.

One of the greatest inventions of all time was the sewn-in tent floor. Before 1960, tents just didn't have floors! Modern campers don't know the perverse pleasures of trying to sleep on the bare ground.

I stuck some Pennyroyal in the ground and crushed some leaves so that the odor would protect us. I intended to go to bed with some of the pungent bush on my chest and around my head. With that in mind I called over to my brother. "Jerry?" I whispered.

"Hunh?" he mumbled.

"Here, catch!"

"Wha...?" he asked.

"Put this around you," I said.

Jerry didn't respond. So I just tossed the little brushy ball of Pennyroyal at him. It hit him softly in the face. Then he exploded! "Yaaaaaaa!" he shrieked, and he leaped up, waving his arms and lifting his feet high to get away from whatever he imagined had attacked him. The tent, of course, collapsed on me! Jerry fled into the woods. Daddy was suddenly interested, saying, "What the hell?" I tried to put the tent back up, but of course I was not a tent man. I held up the poles until Jerry got back, wide awake and looking wild. He clutched his blankets around him and looked at me suspiciously. "What was that?" he rasped. I held up the little ball of Pennyroyal. "You mean this?" I laughed. He just glared at me, grabbed the Pennyroyal and put the tent back up without another word. It started to sprinkle, then to rain, so we both huddled in the tent. Daddy was probably glad that he had a rain flap.

Somehow, we passed the night. The Pennyroyal incident was the climax, of course, but there was a sequel in the morning.

We didn't awake until it was full light. It had stopped raining, but it was still drizzling. Groggily, I looked up to the roof of the tent, and then I froze! Spiders and other bugs and creatures had crept into our tent for shelter, including a thousand mosquitoes who seemed to prefer Pennyroyal to the rain. But they were all quiet, all sleeping. It was a cold, wet, dark morning and they weren't hurting anybody. But they sure scared me!

I poked Jerry, who was always hard to wake up. "Jerry, don't move," I said. "I'm going to get up slowly and leave the tent."

"Huh? Why?" Jerry opened one eye.

"A million things are in here with us, that's why!" I was afraid that Jerry would bolt again, but the daylight must have restored his plainsman's instincts. He and I both crept out of the tent, but at the last second I disturbed one of the flaps and the tent practically took off as the insects came to life! Then we both dashed to the edge of the lake and looked back. Dad sat up, banging his head against the soggy rain flap. "What the hell?" he said.

"The tent," I croaked. "It's full of bugs, spiders and snakes!" The tent lay collapsed, and I'll swear it was moving. Dad and Jerry started laughing.

"Bugs, huh?" Jerry said. He picked up some of the wet, ineffective Pennyroyal. "Here," he said, "This'll keep the bugs off." He wrapped his blanket around him like the Indian he was.

"Maybe not, but it's good for something," I smiled.

"What's that?" Jerry smirked.

"It got you to move pretty fast last night!"

"Hah!," Jerry shot. "Some camper you are!"

And he was right. I would never become a real camper like Dad and Jerry. I wondered if, when Dad was 14 and camping with his Dad in the Ozark wilderness, he had felt the same as I.

Dad just smiled and his eyes twinkled as if he were remembering something. "Someday I'll tell you a story, son," was all he said. The night's discomfort seemed to invigorate Dad as he stretched to greet the new day.

CHAPTER EIGHT

THE OLD MAN

One of Dad's favorite stories was about the Talking Frogs. It is no doubt an old Ozark folk tale and was probably handed down by hill folks. My father told it to me, his Dad to him. It's a story best told around a camp fire. As far as I know, Dad was the first to write the story down. He wrote this story and others in a series of unpublished yarns that he called, "The Old Man." Dad was the Old Man, although the stories were told by a younger fellow who was, I suspect, his alter ego. Dad called this one:

WARNING! FROGS TALKING

You understand this was a special occasion. The old man and I were camped above the high-water mark, that line of trash indicating how high the water had been on its last rampage. Right now we were standing on a gravel bar facing a narrow and deep channel, a "run" as it is called locally, separating two pools, "holes" to you. Across from us the bank rose steeply and the water ran swiftly through the run before entering the pool below. Up-stream I could hear swift water, too. In short, we were between two holes. It was almost sunset and the baby frogs, we called them peepers, were already tuning up for their nightly concert.

Without his usual preamble, the old man began talking. It was faintly annoying to me what with the sense of peacefulness that pervaded the whole picture. Not that I want to give the impression that it was quiet because it wasn't. The water rushing down gave off a loud gurgling sound where it cascaded around the rocks, not a roaring sound but gurgling. It was reassuring. The birds were busy in the trees doing their evening chores. The "peepers" were beginning their concert and once I heard the not to be forgotten call of a lone Whip-poor-will. Yes, it was very peaceful.

"It was here, at the very spot, my Dad and I were standing," began the old man, "yes sir, the very spot." He took a long look around and sighed. "Yes sir, the very same spot, trying to decide where and how we could cross the river. Why we wanted to cross it at all is neither here nor there. We did and that's all. Anyway we stood there all in a puzzlement deciding on whether to go upstream or downstream to find a place to make our crossing.

"Finally Dad said, 'Boy' (he always called me Boy in those days) 'Boy, let's listen to the frogs. They will tell us where we can wade across.'

"I thought it was a crazy idea and said so but Dad insisted and I listened, still thinking it was a fool idea. I didn't have much imagination for interpreting the language of animals in those days. Now, it seems like, I have too much. But to go on, upstream I could hear the peepers sounding off at a great rate. You know, they did sound as if they were saying something in their continual chant. After awhile, when I got tuned in on them you might say, they seemed to be saying, in their high tenor, 'Knee deep! Knee deep! Knee deep!', over and over again.

"Once in the mood, I began to hear more frog talk.

A young batchelor frog across the way sounded off, letting us know in a rich baritone voice that it was, 'Belly deep! Belly deep! Belly deep!' This was turning out to be quite a game, I can tell you.

Carrying the charade a mite further, a close relative, I suppose, in the head of a hole downstream, sounded a warning in a deep bass voice; 'Uh, too deep! Uh, too deep! Uh, too deep!' Still another far down in the middle of the hole gave us the same advice, the voice this time being basso profundo; 'Better go 'round! Better go 'round! Better go 'round - arrrg!' He was a grandpap, I guess.

"That final warning did it. I turned on my heels and headed upstream, Dad following close behind. Sure enough, there was a broad, shallow crossing, a 'riffle' as it is known, barely knee deep, and a trail leading off to somewhere. The peepers had shut up on our approach, of course, but I will never forget the triumphant look on Dad's face as he saw the riffles. Don't tell me that frogs don't talk! I know better. Better listen next time you're out."

Could be.

########

CHAPTER NINE

<u>ON GETTING LOST</u>

Here's another tale told by my Dad, who is the "old man" in the story.

===============

"Speaking about getting lost," said the old man. I tried to remember anything we had said about getting lost but I couldn't. As a matter of fact neither of us had said anything for the last few moments. Of itself that was unusual. Ordinarily the old man was garrulous, hardly waiting to butt in with some comment or other, usually cynical.

As far as I was concerned we were sure of our whereabouts and enjoying the day. Spring was "busting out all over", the up-till-now bare branches of trees showing their first hint of green, the sun warm, the wind quiet (a phenomenon in March), the birds staking out their territory by singing loud and clear and the usual hub-bub of urban life temporariy stilled. The water of the little pond we were walking beside was roily after the recent storm had vented its wrath (and a little water) on the city.

Altogether it was a perfect day for keeping still and listening to Nature's preparations for the season. I guess the old man was aware of that too but he couldn't resist talking for very long so he continued his reminiscence.

"I recollect one time when it was some different from this day. It was right square in the middle of August, the time when the fishin' is poorest, when my Dad asked me would I care about going on a trip with him. He had in mind, he said, to go and look for a 'crick' he had been told about. The fishin' was good even considering the time of year it was, he said, and I believed him. Maybe it was a case of the wish fathering the thought but I was rarin' to go and lost no time in saying so. I told him to give me a half hour to pack our gear and let's go.

"So we went. To make a long story short, I asked where on earth was this place we were heading for in such a hurry. A mite south of here, I was told, someplace called Lost Creek in northern Arkansas. That was the sum total of the information I was given. Oh he did add that it was probable that the whole place was lost in this dry season. The exact words escape me this minute but they were some like this: 'I spect the hull thing is quite lost after the dadgummed drought.' He remarked more cheerfully that the creek was spring fed and carried water year round. With this optimistic statement I relaxed as best I could with the heat and all.

"The next thing I seem to remember, mind you it was a long while ago, we were someplace in Arkansas threading a blacktopped road which suddenly ended in a 'Y', one fork taking off down the valley and the other climbing a steep, rough hill. I recollect we couldn't decide which one was the 'better travelled road', which was the way we used to put it when we were in strange country and came to a fork in the road. Of course there weren't any signs there or any other place either. Folks weren't used to gadding about then.

"The blacktop ended right-dab in front of the fence row marking a property line and there was a neat fieldstone house nestled in the corner. A well-watered garden flourished clear down to the fence which separated us from a man working there.

"As we puzzled about which fork we should take, he came to the fence and said his howdy. Dad said his howdy, too, and asked which fork we should take to get us to Lost Creek.

"He hesitated some while meantime giving us a good going over. He was trying to decide whether he should tell us anything. The natives didn't take kindly to strangers in my day. Sort of like city folks today.

"Anyway, we passed his inspection and he decided to answer Dad's question. I recall the exact words he used, namely, 'Either road will take yuuns thar.' I was particularly interested in that word, 'yuuns', which I had bumped into before on our various jaunts to the hill country. 'Down in the hill country', we used to call it and still do. Want that I should give a lecture on why?" Upon hearing my firm negative response, the old man shrugged and gave me a quizzical look.

"It's the teacher in me, I reckon," he sighed and resumed his yarn. "The hillbilly told Dad that the valley road was a 'mite closer' but it might be wet in some places 'on account of the springs yuuns will have to ford.' It was that phrase, 'mite shorter' that interested Dad. He allowed as how we better take the shortest road in that case. I guess he figured that way we could save some time.

"The next part of the conversation I will never forget. The hill man, with a bit of insight into his own philosophy, said, 'Maybe, but if I was in yuuns place I would go the ridge road. It's farther but a dangsight prettier. Tell me, what are yuuns going to do with the time yuuns is hankering to save after yuuns have saved it? Tell me that, huh?' So after some hemming and hawing on my Dad's part, we took the ridge road after all. It was pretty alright, pretty rough that is, and the hill going down to the village was real scary to me. But after we saw Lost Creek I came to understand what the man meant when he said, '...after yuuns have saved it.'

"Oh, yes, about the fish. We didn't even try after Dad saw what was supposed to be a creek. There were just a couple of stagnant pools and the rest dry creek bed. I was disgusted and even Dad was out of sorts. He said, as I recall it, 'Boy, unpack our bed rolls, build a fire and I will cook our supper. At least we won't be bothered by skeeters tonight. In the morning we'll skedaddle for home by the ridge road, too.'

"Mostly it was a glum ride that day. Dad hummed a song, 'We will take the high road' and every now and then glanced my way. When I was awake he would say, 'We had a good time anyway, didn't we boy?' There wasn't anything I could do but agree with him. I wish now, though, that we had taken the valley road back. It would have saved us time because it was shorter."

"Yes," I reminded him, "but what would you have done with the time after you had saved it?"

The old man actually laughed out loud.

########

CHAPTER TEN

FISHING WITH MOM

In Great Grandmother's day a woman's work was never done. There was heavy work inside and outside the house; feeding the family, cleaning, laundering and gardening. One thing women in those days did not do very often was go fishing. The man of the house still provided all of the food and fishing was food gathering. Later when fishing became recreational, women still didn't fish much because they had no time to waste relaxing.

So the men would say with serious faces, "Well, we'd better get down to the crick and catch tonight's dinner." Then they would go off whistling, preparing to spend the day sitting under a tree.

It took several generations for women to catch on to the real reason their men went fishing. It was not to "catch tonight's dinner" but just to have fun.

By Grandmother's day women were no longer fooled by men's fishing expeditions and they started to go along to see what the fuss was all about.

"You mean all you do is throw that line out there and wait till a fish bites?" Grandma' asked.

"Takes a lot of skill and know-how to be a good fisherman."

"Huh! I could do that."

Grandma decided that two could play that game and she got herself an outfit so she could share the joy.

Grandpa couldn't tell her that one of the reasons a man went fishing was to get away from home. But when Grandma put on her outfit she was so cute Grandpa took her along the next time he went to Lake Tanneycomo.

"Better not get those overalls wet, Mother, they're tight enough already!" Grandpa laughed.

"Well for pity's sake just don't look at me then," Grandma answered and pulled down her straw hat. She took a long cane pole and bucket of worms down to the end of the pier and plopped her ample rear on a folding chair.

You have to understand that Grandma Grace was a Victorian lady with high moral standards. But she was also an adventurer. As one of the Six Singing Smith Sisters of Ohio she had spent ten years doing concerts and entertaining folks in 12 states, including Indian Territory. Their last concert was during the inauguration of President William McKinley, another Ohio native.

So Grandma went fishing to see what the attraction was. She was perfectly willing to get her hands all sloppy with worms and to sit in the dirt. But then she actually caught a fish.

"Oh, now what do I do?" Grandma said as her cane pole jumped up and down in her hands.

"You got one. Pull him in!" Grandpa watched the cane pole with avid interest. The line was moving around in circles as the fish below tried to get away.

Grandma heaved on the pole and the fish, a small bluegill, flew through the air to the dock behind. "Mercy!" Grandma gasped. She walked back to where the little fish was flopping and working its gills.

"Better take him off the hook and throw him back, mother," Grandpa said.

He chuckled as Grandma made a few grabs at the fish.

"Won't you get him off?" she asked.

"That's part of fishing. You have to take care of your own catch." He arched his eyebrows.

So Grandmother finally got hold of the fish, then making noises of disgust she twisted it around trying to work it off of the hook. The bluegill began to bleed and wiggled all the more frantically. She finally dropped the fish, picked up the pole and cast the whole thing back into the water.

"What are you doing?" Grandpa asked.

"The poor thing was bleeding and dying so I put it back in the water.

Grandpa finally hauled the fish out of the water, took it off the hook and threw it back. Then he handed Grandma the pole with a disgusted look.

"Guess I'll wash my hands and go fix lunch," Grandmother said and stalked off, her hips rotating in the overalls like two volley balls stuffed in a bag.

My mother had a more realistic attitude toward fishing. She appreciated the fine art but did not participate except as a cook. She did wonderful things in a skillet with bass, trout and bluegill. When Dad took us to the Lake of the Ozarks, Mom made a big deal about how many fish we might bring back. If we returned empty handed she appeared to be disappointed. She looked upon our fishing trips as food gathering expeditions.

As far as I remember, Mom never wet a line. But she went fishing with us anyway to make sure that we took care of ourselves. She was a great support group.

"Now don't fall in or hook your father," she told us. Dad laughed because we had done both. "Make sure you drink enough water out there in the hot sun."

"Yes, Mother," we said. Mother waved at us as we shoved off, then she went back to our cabin and got out her knitting. Mother might have had the right idea.

In about six hours we were back and Mom was there at the dock to meet us. She always showed the proper enthusiasm for the fish that we caught which we proudly showed her. But she wouldn't clean them.

What happened next was a prime example of the paradox of Mother's personality. Mother came from a hard working but proud family. She had it all together socially and she was very conscious of class. She knew all of the right things to do, which forks to use and what to wear when. She seemed to be a natural born aristocrat.

On the other hand she was a Registered Nurse and as such she was no stranger to the realities of life. She emptied bed pans, gave enemas, cleaned up the sick and was not afraid to plunge into the blood and guts of the emergency room. My sweet, delicate mother!

One summer we were holed up at Twin Bays Resort dodging summer rain showers when the report came from other fishermen that the white bass were running. The fish, sometimes called silver bass and not anything like the black bass, often traveled in large schools and would hit anything thrown at them.

On this day Dad was working and was going to join us on the week-end. Jerry and I begged Mother to let us go out and get some of the silver bass. But Mother was under strict orders not to let us go out in the boat alone. As boat after boat came in with large stringers of the hard-fighting silvers, Mother took a long look at the lake and relented.

"Well, all right, but I'll have to go along in case you get into any trouble."

"You're going fishing with us?" we asked incredulously.

"I'll just put my suit on under my dress and be with you in a minute. Go get the boat ready."

Jerry and I looked at each other. "Great!", Jerry said. We got our fishing gear and went down to the old leaky boat assigned to our cabin. In those days each cabin came with a boat. If you wanted a motor you had to bring your own. It had been raining so we got busy with the bailer and pretty soon we saw Mom coming down the path. She had on a flowered dress and a big hat. It would be embarrassing sitting in the boat with her but we had no choice.

"Cast off!" I ordered and Jerry let go the bow line. I was in the rowing seat, Jerry on the bow and Mother in the stern. The weather looked a little tentative with grey clouds scudding over the lake. But I didn't see any wind action on the water.

Rowing that old wooden scow with three people in it against the wind was hard work. But I had to get us beyond the point and out into fairly deep water. I evened us up about two hundred yards off shore and brought her around. The wind was probably going to blow us in but I figured we could make half a dozen casts before I had to head out again.

I saw no action on the steel grey water, just a running chop. Jerry didn't look too happy about throwing his spoon out into the featureless deep water and Mother had to keep her hand on her hat.

"Let's go get some silvers," I said, and began casting. I had to keep looking around to see how close to shore we were.

"We can't go where the fish are without a motor," Jerry complained. I said nothing but kept on casting.

After half a dozen casts with no response we were getting close to the shore. There was about a 12 inch surf slapping the rocks.

"Why don't we just tie up here, dear?" Mother said.

"Because the fish are out there," I pointed back and started rowing. Jerry let his line out and was trolling as I strained my back rowing away from the shore.

All of a sudden, Jerry went, "Hup!" and pulled back on his rod. "Had a strike." He cast back out and this time the fish slammed his lure just as it hit the water. I shipped the oars and watched, fascinated, as Jerry horsed the fish closer to the boat. It was about a two pound silver.

"Clear the decks!" I yelled, and started casting. We were only about 100 yards from shore and the wind was picking up. Jerry brought his fish in, got it on the stringer and quickly cast back out.

Wham! A big one hit my lure! He was a fighter.

The silver bass jumped about 50 feet away from the boat and I reeled in the slack line. Then Jerry got another one on his line and we were both fighting. I was so excited that I brought my fish in over the stern of the boat and hit Mother right in the face. Blang! Her hat went flying off into the water.

"Oh, my word!" she sputtered and reached for her hat. About that time Jerry stood up at the bow to bring in his fish. The shift in weight made the stern dip down. Mother lost her grip and went right overboard!

Now, here we were catching fish after fish, drifting toward shore at an alarming rate, and our Mother is floundering around in the water, her dress blossoming like a giant water lily. "Help! Help!", she screeched.

I dropped my rod with the fish still on it and manned the oars. In the bow, Jerry was still standing up fighting his fish. When the boat lurched throwing Mom in the water, Jerry lost his balance and fell out of the boat too! But Jerry was pretty quick; he grabbed the boat with one hand, and the other still held his rod.

"Go help Mom," I shouted. Somehow, Jerry dropped his rod in the bottom of the boat with the fish still hooked. The reel handle miraculously caught on a seat and the line stayed tight.

Jerry was working his way up to the stern of the boat, puffing and blowing and Mother was still dog paddling. Even though they were both floundering in the water and the wind was picking up, I couldn't stand it so I retrieved Jerry's rod and landed his fish. Meanwhile, Jerry had grabbed Mom.

"I gotcha," he said and heaved her into the boat. Mother lay sprawled head down, in close proximity to the fish that had hit her in the face. Then Jerry pulled himself into the boat, spewing water, just as the boat crunched ashore on the rocks.

"Where's my fish?" he sputtered.

"I got it!" I yelled. Then I shoved off of the rocks and started to row down the shore. It began to rain harder. It turned into a downpour and soon I was as wet as Jerry and Mom. They sat huddled in the stern as I heaved at the oars and fought the wind and waves. After what seemed like forever we rounded the point into calmer waters and headed for the Twin Bays dock. There was someone standing there watching us.

It was Dad!

"What the hell?" was the first thing he said. He might have been angry but the sound of his voice and his strength as he pulled us from the boat gave me a great sense of security.

Later as we sat around the fire wrapped in blankets Mom chirped about how brave we were. She said that Jerry had saved her and I was very good with the oars. Jerry smiled but he was no doubt thinking about all those fish out there which he hadn't caught. Mom didn't say anything about being hit in the face with a fish or losing her hat.

"Well, at least you got some good fish," Dad said, holding up the stringer. "Just enough for dinner. Maybe if it quits raining we can go out and get some more."

Neither Jerry or I wanted to admit to being scared, exhausted and temporarily discouraged, so we both just frowned at him.

"Just kidding," Dad said. "Well, you know the rules. You catch 'em, you clean 'em." He held up the stringer to us.

"Not this time," Mom said with a strange tone in her voice. "I guess if I can fall out of the boat and get rescued in a hurricane the least I can do is clean the fish these boys took so **much trouble to catch.**"

"Thanks, Mom," I said. "I'll buy you a new hat."

########

CHAPTER ELEVEN

WET CAMP

This is Dad's yarn about a trip he took with brother Jerry. According to this, Jerry just "knew" all of those woodsman's tricks. Dad left out the fact that he himself was the woodsman and that Jerry had learned all of his lore from Dad.

The old man was fit to be tied, to use one of his expressions, while I was telling my tale about being on a wet camping trip. He constantly shifted his position on the bench, made frequent interruptions and otherwise made known his anxious wishes to recount his own past experiences.

"Talk about wet camps! Huh! Wait till you hear about one I've had - among others - I should say."

This was the only reaction I received in response to my yarn. I should have suspected it. When the old man wished to talk he did so at the first opportunity. So, I waved my hand to signify he had the right of way, although I did so reluctantly.

"Well, let's see now. How did it all happen? Now that you have shown a willingness to listen for a change, I'm bound to remember it. Oh, yes, I've got it. My middling boy and I set out on a fishin' trip in mid-summer. The trip was a spur of the moment thing. Both of us were home at the same time for once and I said to him, 'How about the two of us going fishing?' Well, he jumped at the chance. I guess his fever was as high as mine was; fishin' fever I mean. Anyway, it was a perfect day, one of those you dream about. It was hot and clear with no wind, not even a breeze.

"It was too perfect, you know, a calm before the storm sort of thing. My mother would have said it was a 'weather breeder", but she was always a pessimist. Me, I take after my Dad in this regard. He was a hopeless optimist. He always said that he had more fun being an optimist in that he could anticipate with pleasure more things than a pessimist could. But I have seen him chewing his lip many times when he was worried about something. But to get back to fishin'.

"As I was saying, we lit out and on the way I outlined my plans. The boy, of course, was agreeable. I planned to rent a boat, pack our gear in it and head for an island I knew. It was there we would pitch camp.

"Well, everything went dandy at first. The car purred along, the traffic was light and I was as relaxed as any person should be who is going fishin'. The first hint of possible trouble brewing was when I spotted a big cloud on the horizon. But I discounted that. There are lots of clouds and who knows what a cloud will do in mid-summer? Usually they drift away or disappear before they can pose a threat. I reasoned that this cloud was one of those harmless ones and I didn't let it bother me. You know how it is. I was rarin' to go fishin' and in that mood a feller isn't apt to be bothered by anything.

"By and by we got to the lodge, as it was called in those by-gone days. It calls itself a 'marina' now-a-days. I got us a boat, packed our gear in it and covered it with a ground cloth that the kid had insisted we take along. Bless his heart!

"It was a happy thought as it turned out. Me, I wouldn't have thought of that, since I never did use one. But as it turned out we sure needed it! The boy climbed in the boat, I launched it and started the putt-putt and just then we heard a boom of thunder not far off. But we didn't pay any heed to it, eager as we were, and began the short trek to the island. By the time we cleared the bay the wind struck us. It pretty near turned us around. Dang! We had run head-on into a summer squall! The lake was full of whitecaps already so I lost no time in quartering the boat bankside to the waves. Even then it was slow going. When I think back on it I'm tempted to say 'dang' again. And the rain began! It was a slanting rain, ice cold it was, and in a minute we were soaked. Of course we had our 'Mae Wests' on but they did little to keep us dry. The kid promptly tucked the ground cloth about our duffle again and both of us drew our hats down low on our faces and kept going. That's the amazing thing about it. Nowa-days I would turn back. But that's the way it was in those days when I was younger. The boy was having a great time, I guess, and I must admit I was too. Sounds stupid to you? Yeah, I reckon so. Even so we managed to buck our way to the island."

Though I had not said a word, the old man read my glance and assumed, rightly, what my thoughts were.

"But it was a brief squall, though it didn't seem like one when the rain was stinging our faces and the waves were threatening to capsize the boat. By the time we beached the boat on the island the sunball was shining on the trees which were still dripping on us. Tiny rivulets raced through the gravel and on the whole it was very wet.

"Then it was that the kid demonstrated his know-how. While I was securing the boat he sloshed around looking for a less-wet spot where we could camp. He finally chose a big log and was already attempting to roll another big log sideways to it. He did it, too! The result was to create a right angle, in the corner of which he planned to build his campfire. He explained that the logs would reflect heat, would catch fire and smoulder through the night, thus providing heat. I was right proud of the right angle and the plan for the fire, though I wouldn't know about the last part. As far as I was concerned those logs didn't provide much heat.

"In the meantime the duffle was carried up and I stood around waving my arms and offering to help. Know what the kid did then?

Well he had the gall to order his own father to select some flat rocks to be placed as sort of a fireplace. This done, I scurried around bringing dead limbs so that he could peel the bark and reveal dry wood. At least that was the general idea but I'll admit that it was an optimistic one at that. The boy shaved a bunch of thin slices of wood and very neatly piled them into a sort of tepee. But when he tried to light them all we got was smoke. Though he huffed and puffed, the fire only smoldered until I got the one constructive idea I'd had all day. I scrounged around trying to locate some dry rags to soak in gasoline. Dry rags were hard to come by but finally I located a couple and my idea worked.

"But golly that fire felt good! The boy dug some trenches to guide the rivulets away, I went through our foodstuffs, spread the cover cloth near the fire and started to prepare supper. In the meantime the sun-ball disappeared behind a cloud, the wind came up and the rain came again! This meant that everything I'd done had to be done over again. So be it, I done it again. The rain turned out to be a clearing-up shower and although we shivered, the smoldering fire helped to warm us some.

"Though the rain was just a goodbye shower, it was heavy enough to make the rivulets start sluicing again. It was most discouraging. How-some-ever we were mighty hungry and so we went on with our preparations for supper. Do you know how to make a wet camp wetter? I'll tell you. I put the coffee pot on a supposedly flat rock and the dadgummed rock tilted, spilling water over the fire, our one remaining comfort. Boy, was I disgusted! The boy, though, took it as a matter of course. He rebuilt the fire - luckily there was still some burning - and did other chores all the time whistling! I guess he was trying to keep my morale up, or his own.

"Well to make a short story shorter, we ended up with a very snug wet camp. We took our wet shoes and put them close to the fire. Partially dry, warm shoes are more comfortable than cold and wet ones. We dug our 'hip holes' and wrapped our blankets, them as were dry, around us and tried to get some sleep. You ask about fishin'? Man, it never occurred to us that evening! In the morning I made a half-hearted attempt but the fish didn't cooperate.

"So we caught nothing, but maybe a cold. For once, though, I wasn't ashamed to go home without fish."

"Is that it?" I asked. The old man merely smiled. "Are you trying to tell me that you were totally helpless because of a little rain and that your boy showed all of the brilliance of Daniel Boone and did all the work?"

At that the old man frowned a little. He shrugged his shoulders and started to say something but instead he just smiled and there was a twinkle in his eye.

I looked at him and said, "I guess when you're an old man you can get away with just about any lie."

"Look who's talkin'," he said as he lit his pipe.

########

CHAPTER TWELVE

THE COPPERHEAD

I never saw a real live coiled rattlesnake up close, although I have been in places where such an encounter would be possible. Contact was avoided because I was always cautious and prepared. I once saw a whole ball of rattlesnakes blasted into the sky at a rock quarry, landing where I did not care to know. But through the years rattlers and I were successful in avoiding each other and I hope it stays that way.

Copperheads were a different matter. Arrogant and well-armed, they were the vipers we feared most when we were kids in Missouri. Copperheads sometimes didn't even bother to coil up and hiss before they struck. They were definitely bad guys.

I had nothing personal against copperheads, but they seemed to dislike me intensely. It was, "strike on sight" when they saw me. If a rattler spotted you, he'd slither away and hide, hoping you would leave his territory. A rattler only attacks in self-defense. But a copperhead was always looking for trouble. If you came within his territory, it was "battle stations" for him and all of his relatives. "There's Dave! Get him! Get him!" It was as if snakes hundreds of miles apart had somehow communicated and had issued "wanted" posters. I was a "wanted man" among all copperheads.

Actually, there might have been some reason for this. Since copperheads were so arrogant, I adopted a "shoot first" policy myself. I would go copperhead hunting with a big stick, a rifle and a Bowie knife. Since I was only about 12 at the time, the weapons sometimes outweighed my body. In those days I looked like the 98-pound weakling in the 1938 Charles Atlas muscle ads.

Copperheads are where you find them. You might well expect to meet one in the woods or in a wilderness rock pile. But you wouldn't expect to find one in what was then suburban Columbia, Missouri, out by the M.U. Agricultural Experimental Farm. The little snakes we encountered in the woods along Hinkson Creek were more afraid of us than we were of them. Jerry and I spent many hours playing Jessie James or World War One in those woods.

There was an abandoned quarry around there somewhere which we had been warned not to go near. But one day we just ran onto it while romping around with our cap pistols. We crossed the creek on some rocks and scrambled up a bank. And suddenly there it was.

Rusty, iron-colored rocks fell in jagged profusion down the quarry sides. The blue-green water at the bottom of the pit must have been very deep. We kicked rocks down the side and watched them splash into the emerald water. The quarry reminded me of a giant ant lion hole and I expected something to come leaping out of it.

Walking along the bank looking down into the quarry, we came to an area where the most recent work had been done. The bank ended in rough rock slabs. We climbed around and over the rocks for a while and finally decided that we'd better go back.

I turned around to climb up over a rocky ledge. I had just pulled myself up to the top when I came face to face with a coiled copperhead! He was six inches away from my nose! All I could see was that diamond shaped head drawn back and ready to strike.

I ducked and the snake shot off into space. He must have been coiled on some loose gravel. He was so mad that he didn't even look to see where he was striking. I looked over my shoulder and saw the snake bounce off of the rocks below and fall into the green water. If I wasn't so scared, I would have laughed. Jerry did laugh.

"It's a copperhead!" I yelled, trying to scare Jerry into the proper attitude. "Probably another one up here so be careful." Jerry scrambled up beside me and we both saw the other one at the same time. He was mottled brown like the rocks and looked at us suspiciously. We threw rocks at him and jumped up and down. But instead of slithering away, the darn snake started right for us. Fortunately, we were faster than the copperhead and we managed to get back over the creek without once looking back.

A copperhead will strike at anything within range. It doesn't matter if it is only a board or a stick. If the snake thinks it is the least bit threatened, he will try to shoot venom into a rock.

We saw this one evening down at Dad's camp at Lake Ozark. We were walking to our cabin along a neat path bordered with white rocks. We were practically there when I saw what looked like a brown stick. Then the stick, about 8 inches long, moved! It was an adolescent copperhead, which launched itself in unbridled rage at my boot. It struck twice before my boot took care of him. The copperhead lay there, a smashed would-be killer, its fangs dripping and its head twitching. It was so little it looked more like a long worm. It was amazing how vicious the thing was, even though we were not in any way threatening it.

Dad picked the snake up with a stick and carried it back to the cabin. Once there we said "hi" to Mom and laid the snake on the table. "What on earth is that?" Mom said suspiciously.

"Just a dead snake," Dad told her.

"On my table?" Mother looked disgusted.

"Just for a minute. We don't get a chance to see a copperhead up close very often."

"Look at those beady little eyes," I said, "and those vicious fangs." Then, as I was looking very closely at the snake, it leaped into the air! It hit me in the face! I jumped a foot. "Wow," I howled, "Am I bit? Am I bit?"

Everybody else had jumped back when the snake moved and Jerry looked like he was about ready to leave the room. But it was just some kind of a muscle spasm, a left-over chemical that had caused a reaction in a nerve somewhere. The snake was good and dead. But even in death, the little copperhead was capable of generating fear.

I went to my room about then to change my underpants!

########

CHAPTER THIRTEEN

WHAT DID HE SAY?

Birds and animals always seem to be saying something to those sensitive enough to hear it. Our Dad was one of the best at figuring out what the wildlife were saying. He probably got the trick from his dad, the one who knew about talking frogs.

"No, Dadgummit, we're not!" I heard Dad say. We were tied up fore and aft onto the shady bluff shore of the river and had been since shortly after noon.

"Who are you talking to?" I asked.

"Him," Dad said, motioning up to a tree. "Did you hear what he said?"

"What?"

"He said, plain as day, 'Ketchin any? Ketchin any?' Listen to him!" Dad was plenty grumpy after a whole day without fish. He'd been up at dawn, working the long hole first with his fly rod, then with a bait casting rod and now with live bait. We hadn't had a strike all day.

The bird tweetered again but it didn't say anything to me. "Hear that?" Dad said.

"Yeah. He said 'Let's go home. Let's go home.'"

There was more than one bird that said things to Dad. A redbird said, "What cheer? What cheer?" Robins said, "Cheer up! Cheer up!" A hootowl said, "Who? Who? Who cooks for you?" And of course there was the bobwhite and whippoorwill. Their songs formed those words plainly. But sometimes these same birds said different things to Dad. A bobwhite would fly over and say, "Hold tight! Hold tight!." Whippoorwills sometimes said, "Poor Bill! Poor Bill!" or "Whip your pole! Whip your pole!" Another time a bird would fly right over Dad on a hot, sunny day and say, "Thirsty? Thirsty?"

But there was one bird that didn't say anything in English to Dad. It was a big crow, but instead of saying, "Caw!" this one would say something like, "Rain! Rain!" I could never pick it up, but Dad did.

"Storm's comin'," he would say.

"How do you know?"

"Just heard a rain bird." And sure enough, in about an hour it would rain.

I asked Dad once where he got all these ideas about what the birds were saying.

"It seems to me that's what they're saying. But I guess it's like seeing faces and things in clouds. Just your imagination."

About that time a big heron rose mightily from its nest on an island. It sounded like a British destroyer's whooping siren. "What's he saying now?" I asked Dad.

"Danged if I know." Dad could be obtuse. "But let me tell you about a time when I was fishing with my dad down on Taneycomo. You know, dad was not always a preacher. He did his share of odd jobs and he was part owner of a grocery store that he ran for years. He didn't go into the preaching business until after I came along. I wish I'd have known him when he wasn't a preacher because he was a pretty great guy without all of the "God" stuff."

"Didn't you approve of his calling?" I asked.

"I somehow suspected that he wasn't really a preacher. It was the way he acted when he wasn't in church. Sometimes the stories he told weren't exactly preacher-like. And that day on the lake I was almost sure that he was going to give it up and get a real job!"

"What happened?"

"It was one of those birds I've been telling you about. Your grandpa was even better than I about knowing what the birds were saying. He would constantly be talking to one. 'No, we're not!' Or, 'I'll use you for bait if you don't shut up.' I didn't pay much attention or comment any because I could see the old man was getting testy. He was frowning and throwing his lures impatiently. He didn't act that way very often but it had been a trying day. First he couldn't get his old outboard to work. He had to keep putting the pull rope on and yanking it off. Then he threw off the tip of his rod and though he got it back it needed repairs. Sitting around camp on a hot afternoon trying to fix a rod tip wasn't his idea of fun. When we finally got back out on the lake, we didn't get any strikes."

"Sounds like some of our days," I said.

"Yeah, but we're not preachers. It was harder on him because he wasn't supposed to lose his temper. He was constantly aware that the Lord might be testing him."

"So what happened?"

"He must have been testing him all right because pretty soon Dad got hung up in a tree. It was one of his best lures and he didn't want to lose it. He thrashed around quite a bit but the tree wouldn't let loose. So We went in to get it. It was just out of reach.

'Well, son, what are we going to do?' Dad asked.

'Maybe a little prayer wouldn't hurt,' I said.

'I'm not sure the Lord is happy with me today,' he said. With that he hopped ashore onto a little bluff under the tree. He reeled the line in as far as he could. Then he bent the tree down as far as he could and he almost reached it. About that time a big blue bird swooped in and landed in the tree. 'I suppose you're going to help,' Dad said. And the bird kind of hunched its shoulders up and down and shrieked, 'Kee-rist!

Kee-rist!' Well, I thought Dad was going to fall off that bluff. He was so startled by what the bird had said that he just let go of the tree and the line and everything. He got down on his knees and said, 'Lord, if that's you, please help me get this lure out of the tree.' And the plug fell right out of the tree and onto the rock in front of Dad."

"I'm sure it was the relaxing of the line that did it, but you couldn't tell Dad that. The bird flew away after the tree sprang back like a tripped snare. But ever after that whenever Dad heard a bluejay screech, 'Kee-rist', he would look up and say, 'Thank you Lord, I'll try to remember that.' He was quite a man."

It's nice to know that sensitivity like that can be inherited. Dorothea and I were fishing with Jerry's kids on the Lake of the Ozarks. One morning the kids were out early and reported that they had heard a "Dorothea" bird.

"What the heck kind of bird is that?" I asked.

"I don't know, but we heard this bird singing and it sounded like, 'Dor-thee-uh! Dor-thee-uh!'"

Later I went out with them and heard what they called the "Dorothea" bird, but it just sounded like a redbird to me. I guess some people have it and some people don't.

########

CHAPTER FOURTEEN

BAIL! BAIL!

Most old wooden fishing boats leaked a little. Even when they didn't they could collect plenty of water when left tied to open docks during thunder storms. Those old wooden boats had to be bailed out so frequently that a rusty tin can bailer was usually standard equipment, along with an anchor stone attached to a 20 foot rope.

Old wooden fishing boats had character. Their seats produced splinters. The motor mount at the stern was chewed-up, greasy and of uncertain strength. The bow of the boat was often stove-in, split or otherwise damaged from collisions with rocks, docks and perhaps other boats. But no matter how battered they were those old wooden fishing boats would never sink, even when encouraged to do so, as I am about to relate.

It was a summer afternoon in 1944 and my Uncle Pic was home after the greatest adventure of his life as a MASH surgeon with the

82nd Airborne in World War II. That War wasn't over but Pic's war was. And now he was going fishing with his family on the new Grand Lake of the Cherokees.

To me, Uncle Pic and Aunt Francis Darrough and their beautiful kids were remarkable people. They combined professionalism with aristocracy, creativity with horse sense. They had taste, they had class and they could buy things. To me they were romantic.

Pic Darrough was another man born too late. His father, W.H. Darrough, had been a U.S. Marshal when Oklahoma was still Indian Territory. Pic wanted to be a cowman or a sheriff. He liked wide open spaces and dusty towns. He was a dead shot with either hand. He rode horses and bulls and he had a look in his eye that made men think twice before talking back to him.

But times had changed. Law and order had come to Oklahoma. And Pic's mother didn't raise him to be a gun-fighter. Unfortunately for his wilderness heart, Pic was brilliant, so he went to medical school. When he finished he married my Mother's sister, Francis, who was a nurse, and they both went to work at Oklahoma State Hospital.

Soon he was Chief of Surgery and a respected member of the medical fraternity. I should point out that all I know about Pic before I met him is hearsay. But I saw enough of him later to know that most of what I had heard was true.

When I met Pic he was a ranch owner, cattle baron, story teller, dead shot, country doctor and a compulsive drinker in a dry state! Medicine was his life, but it wasn't enough for him. Pic needed controlled violence. He always wanted to hit something, shoot something, win something. When he wasn't busy with a scalpel, he was playing with a rope or his .38.

The Cherokee dam had only been finished for a short time and the big lake they would call the Grand Lake of the Cherokees was still filling. Pic was very proud of the new lake, which he considered Oklahoma's answer to Missouri's Lake of the Ozarks. The lake was filling slowly and the valleys and hills with their brown grasses and yellow wild flowers went under water almost imperceptibly.

On one hill, where they later built a fishing cabin, the Darroughs had a camp site. The map showed a road going right to it, but now the road was under water. The water was filling a little draw on both sides of the campsite and later it would be a peninsula. Right now there was no way to get to it except by boat.

We drove down to the end of the road where it went into the water. This was the end of the line. We all piled out of two cars and began unloading equipment. There were eight of us - Mom and Dad, Pic and Francis, Jerry and me, Nancy and Mary Beth. There was the usual 100 pounds of equipment and one flashlight. Pic had hauled an old wooden 14-footer behind his Ford. Pic and Dad floated the boat and Pic checked out the new 25 horse outboard he had just bought. He secured it to the motor mount, yanked the cord and it roared to life.

"Looks a little too powerful for a boat like that," Dad said.

"Well, it's a heavy boat," Pic said, and started loading the tents and cook pots.

Mom, Dad and Pic got in first and Pic piloted the craft across the short draw to the campground. After unloading, Pic returned for us. Meanwhile, we were all jumping around and showing off for our beautiful cousins. Pic started barking orders and getting us organized. We loaded the boat with food, water, tackle, rods, and then the six of us. With all that gear and all of us, the boat rode rather low in the water.

It wasn't very far across the draw, but instead of paddling, Pic started his powerful engine. "Cast off!" he yelled, and the boat lept ahead. The motor roared, the boat surged, then the bow headed straight down!

"Stop the motor!" we yelled. "The boat's going under!" The overloaded old boat was filling. "Bail! Bail!" everybody shouted as Pic stopped the motor. But with what? I looked around frantically. I saw nothing but a half gallon can full of sugar. I emptied it overboard and started bailing.

"Nobody move!" Pic said quietly. I started bailing. Others looked around and began bailing with containers they had emptied of what were no doubt necessities for our survival. Right then, nobody cared. We bailed tons of water from the boat, but the old hulk stayed practically awash.

As a matter of fact, the boat had already sunk. By itself, it probably would not have gone under, even with all that water in it. But with all the gear and all of us, just a little more water would have put it down. So we bailed and bailed, while Mom and Dad looked questioningly at us from the far shore.

"What's the matter," Dad yelled. "Can't start the motor?"

"Nevermind," Pic yelled. "We'll be right over." Even Pic had started to bail, using the empty gas can. The water around us began to look like a garbage dump while the boat slowly raised its gunwales above the surface. Eventually, we made it over to the camp site by paddling and bailing. Dad pulled the boat in and started laughing. "What the hell?"

"The motor pushed her right under," Pic explained. "And we had to dump most of the food to bail the boat."

Dad continued to laugh until he heard that all the sugar was gone. He liked sugar in his coffee.

We spent the rest of the evening setting up camp and laughing around. I had been on many a fishing trip with Dad and Jerry and even with Mom, but never with two such pretty girls as Nancy and Mary Beth. It was a romantic fantasy come true. Both Jerry and I didn't act quite sane as we discussed where we would sleep and what we would do tomorrow.

But then the bubble burst. It turned out that Pic had to work that night and the girls had summer school. They were just with us for the afternoon and for supper. After dinner all the Darroughs were going home for the night. They would be back the next afternoon to go fishing with us. Then when we went to make dinner we found there was nothing to eat but canned beans, bacon and some canned peaches. Everything else had gone overboard when the boat almost sank.

We waved goodby as the now lightened boat zipped across the cove to the darkening shore. I realized that to get the boat back, one of us would have to swim over there in the morning and get it. I tried not to think about who that would be.

After they left, Dad sat at the campfire, drinking his sugarless coffee. It seemed to make him bitter as he made a noise and threw it on the ground.

"O.K., kids, I'll help you get your tent up," Dad said. He put the old World War One shelter halves together and hung them over a rope he had tied between two trees. Jerry, always handy, tied the tent ropes to stakes and hammered them into the ground. The result was a pleasingly taut shelter over some suspicious-looking ground. The ground cloth went over that and our bed rolls were thrown in to finish the job.

We sat around the fire for a lttle while, then mother went to bed. I peeked into their 12-foot wall tent. Mother and Dad had army cots neatly tucked next to the high walls of the tent. I immediately felt envious, and I must have looked like it. "What's the matter?" Dad asked. "You wouldn't expect your Mother to sleep on the ground, would you?"

"Looks pretty comfortable," I said peevishly.

"Go on to bed," Dad grinned. "I know you guys like to rough it."

We roughed it, all right. Neither the ground cloth nor the bed roll was enough to keep the rocks and creepy-crawly Oklahoma bugs from interfering with my sleep. Jerry went right out, but I lay there apprehensively, wondering what the peculiar odor was. It smelled kind of like wet hay.

Morning came mercifully and gave me an excuse to get up and out of that cursed shelter tent. Jerry continued to snooze. It was cold and damp and the fire was out. But I no longer smelled wet hay, and the rocks no longer punished by body.

I looked forward to a great day. We would go fishing, the pretty Darrough girls would be back this afternoon. Then, we would all go home and sleep in real beds.

It wasn't until we were breaking camp that I discovered our tent had been placed right over a bunch of old cow pies! When we told Dad about his unfortunate choice of a site for our shelter because of the cow pies, he just grinned.

I have wondered ever since if he put the tent there on purpose because I had dumped all the sugar into the lake. Of course, it was probably just an accident.

########

CHAPTER FIFTEEN

THE MAN WITH SILVER BULLETS

Dad was older than Pic Darrough by 5 or 6 years. He was a more experienced fisherman than Pic and he had two boys. Pic had two girls, rode horses and knew more about guns than Dad and that sort of made them even.

When these two got together on a fishing trip it was the Mountain Man against the Plains Drifter. Sometimes it was hard to tell whether their roughhousing was serious or just noisy fun.

Pic had a heart of gold but he didn't like anybody to be better at anything than he was. It was not enough for Pic to think that he was the best. He needed to demonstrate and test the fact whenever possible. So here came my dad, a big bear of a man who was unexpectedly quick on his feet, only a fair shot but a great fisherman. Dad had married Pic's wife's older sister and had produced, so far, two boys.

Pic probably wouldn't have wanted to compete so much with an older guy except that Dad had something that Pic really wanted - not just one but two boys! And "all" Pic had produced were girls. Somehow Pic thought it took a real he-man to produce boys and it disturbed him to think that he might not be as much of a man as was Dad. It was ridiculous, of course, but Pic was from the old school. I don't know what Dad thought but since he already had his boys he was probably smug about it.

So Pic set out to see what Dad was made of. He tried to beat him in macho contests with fishing, guns, horses and whiskey.

As I have said, Dad was a fair shot. He was trained in the R.O.T.C. and was a sharp-shooter with a 30-06. But Pic's forte was hand guns. He mostly used a 32 caliber Smith & Wesson double-action 6-shooter. He had heavier caliber pistols but he liked the .32 because it didn't recoil as much and he could just spray his target with fair control.

Dad had a big .38 special. It was Spanish American War military issue and was probably declared surplus after the Army adopted the .45 automatic. The .38 special was almost as powerful as the .45

because of its extra powder load. But it only held six shots and was slower to fire. Dad's .38 had quite a recoil but it was old and worn. Instead of kicking up and to the right like most guns, his bucked down and to the left! Of course if you knew how the pistol would recoil you could control its accuracy. But once you got used to Dad's old .38 it was hard to shoot a normal gun.

We were out fishing one day and Pic decided it would be fun to sink some empty beer cans with gunfire. Pic watched Dad sink three cans with his .38 while Pic only holed one with his .32.

"Give me that gun, Uncle Pic," I said. Pic looked startled but he handed it over to me. I quickly sank the other two cans. This would never do so Pic loaned Dad one of his guns, claiming it would make the contest more equal if they both used the same kind of piece. Sure enough, Dad's shooting was not as accurate with the little .32, although I continued to do fairly well with it. But Pic wasn't interested in how good a shot I was. He wanted to beat Dad!

"Let's go ashore and get a drink," Pic said, "and I'll show you some real shooting." Now, I'm not saying that Pic cheated, but what he did made it easier for him to win. The contest was just between him and Dad and they both used .32 double actions.

After the target shoot was over and the scores all tabulated showing Pic the winner, Dad picked up his old .38 and blew the target away with two shots. Then he went out on the lake and caught two nice Bass for dinner.

After Dad's third son was born and Pic's third daughter arrived the competition got rough. Of course, we didn't know any of this at the time. We would see some of the macho by-play. Pic ragged Dad from the plains of Oklahoma to the Missouri Ozarks and as far as I know Dad held his own most of the time. Then came the war - World War Two. Dad was back with the government and Pic was growing beef and had started to wear a big .38 on his hip. He was still doing house calls and on the way he would practice with the big gun by blowing away road signs. Sometimes he would go off the road and take a short cut across the plains. On those occasions he would shoot at anything that moved. It must have been quite a picture; Pic's old Ford 2-door bouncing across the open fields, dust billowing up behind it, gun smoke coming out of the windows, herds of jack rabbits, coyotes and gophers running ahead of the car. I don't have any reports on body counts.

It was about this time that Pic started using .38 special bullets with chrome casings. He showed me some of those shells once and I started calling him the man with silver bullets. Pic was proud of that gun and when he enlisted in the 82nd Airborne he asked permission and it was granted for him to carry the .38 with the "silver bullets" as his own personal weapon.

Pic gave it one more try before he went off to war. He and Francis invited us to visit that summer and he pulled out all the stops. First there was a rodeo where Pic sponsored one of the bull rides. Pic didn't ride the bull, but I'm sure he identified with it.

Then we went out to Pic's ranch, where he wanted us to ride horses and go out with the cows. Fortunately Mother vetoed that for us but Dad had no excuse. So he swung up on one of Pic's cow ponies and went loping, or rather bouncing, off with Pic. I could see Pic looking back with a funny smile on his face to see if Dad was alright. Then they disappeared in the dust.

We stood around kicking dirt at the other cows and running back behind the fence when the cattle looked annoyed. The next thing I knew Pic and Dad were back. Dad was leaning over his horse's neck and his hand had been wrapped in an old bandanna. Pic swung off his horse. "Horse stepped on his thumb," he said, pulling Dad off. "Got to get him to the clinic. Francis, you drive the boys home. Clarice, you come with us. Let's go." Dad looked pale and in pain, but he winked at me as he and Mom got in Pic's car and roared off.

Later we heard the grim details. Dad's horse had stopped suddenly because of a snake or something but Dad didn't stop. He went right over the horse's head and landed in a rocky draw like a sack of potatoes. While he was trying to get up, the horse jumped over the draw and came down on his thumb. It was mashed pretty bad. Dad was lucky that he had one of the world's best doctors to take care of him. On the other hand, you could say that if it hadn't been for Pic, Dad wouldn't have been aboard that skittish horse in the first place.

Of course, Pic did everything he could to fix Dad's hand. He would not have wanted Dad to get really hurt for the world. Pic was probably just hoping that his tenderfoot pal would have a little trouble with the horse and have to be rescued. As far as I know Dad never rode a horse again after that.

Pic became a line surgeon in the 82nd Airborne. He trained like every other trooper. In jump school Pic was reportedly more enthusiastic than his buddies about leaping out of planes. He continued drinking but as usual he could never take more than one or two swallows before throwing up. He didn't want the boys to know that he couldn't drink so he raised a lot of hell. I heard that once he fired off a whole clip from a B.A.R. in a company street and they put him in the stockade for the night.

The day came when the 82nd shipped out for Sicily but Pic didn't get his orders. He was in the clinic with a violent skin rash on his hands. He couldn't function as a doctor or anything else with that rash so they kept him home until it cleared up. The 82nd got to Sicily and became a victim of one of the war's worst friendly fire goofs. The 504th combat team, arriving over the beachhead only an hour after a Nazi air raid, was shot out of the sky by nervous navy gunners and shore batteries.

Pic came to see us just before he re-joined the 82nd in England. He asked me what service I was going into. I said I had been thinking about the navy.

"The navy!" he snarled. "Those blind stupid jerks!" He told us how the navy had shot down a lot of his friends. He wouldn't acknowledge that it was a mistake. Later Pic landed in France with support units of the 82nd. They were one of the first outfits to liberate Dachau and Lt. Colonel Pic Darrough was one of the first doctors in there. The experience changed Pic forever. After seeing the horrors of that camp all of the bravado kind of drained out of Pic. After he came home he seemed to have an entirely different attitude toward life. For one thing he quit competing with Dad and began to enjoy their quiet fishing trips.

To Jerry and me Pic was one of the greatest characters who ever lived. He was like the hero in every Western ever made. He was strong, reliable and dedicated to mankind. He had a statesman-like attitude toward Native Americans and he hated injustice.

Pic also had a heroic attitude toward himself. He once set his own broken ankle, then drove 300 miles to a hospital. Another time he cut himself badly and sewed up his own wound. Pic had old fashioned attitudes about right and wrong, honor and glory, men and women.

They don't make 'em like Pic Darrough anymore.

########

CHAPTER SIXTEEN

TO BUILD A FIRE

<u>This is another of Dad's "Old Man" stories which he wrote in a fictional format but which were based on true events.</u>

We were sitting, the old man and I, alongside a small stream which burbled sleepily to itself. Close by a group of Boy Scouts was practicing its newly found skill of fire building; tepee, log cabin and various other types. I noticed the old man paying particular attention to one boy who was attempting to build his fire "log cabin" style. When he began to stuff dry leaves and twigs into it, I heard the old man snort loudly. With this, I turned my head and he nodded in the direction of the boy.

"Reminds me of the time when I'd just learned to build a fire like that one. I was a little tad then and I'd just passed my fire building exam with the Boy Scouts. Man, was I proud. My chance to try it for real came when my Dad asked me would I like to go with him on an afternoon fishing jaunt. Of course I was dead anxious to go, so we went. Dad allowed as how we would be back home that night, that I wouldn't need the sleeping outfits and when I'd carried the supper foodstuffs to the car he was ready to go.

"Despite Dad's usual haphazard driving, we reached our destination within the hour. Dad drove the old bus smack-dab to the river front and pointed to our setting down place. We disembarked and after stretching his legs, Dad took off with his minnow trap leaving me to unload the rest of the equipment.

In those days, Dad fished with long cane poles.

"It was my job to unscramble the assortment of lines, hooks, sinkers, lures and bobbers attached to the poles. Being a little kid, this kind of procedure was unfamiliar to me and I made a mess of it. I suppose that when I was real little, my Dad taught me to fish with cane poles like that, but I don't remember it. As far as I knew, I had never fished with a cane pole before. And I've never done it since. I have to tell you something about it if you don't mind."

I didn't mind and I said so. Besides, I was interested in the cane poles. I couldn't imagine the old man fishing with old-fashioned cane poles. So I made myself comfortable and proceeded to listen.

"Eager like, I shouldered my pole and headed for a pool which I thought we were going to fish. Was I ever surprised when Dad took off in the other direction! But there he went. He looked like a sporting goods store going somewhere. Except in my mind's eye I don't have a picture of him walking away. I wish I did." He sighed and continued. "In one hand he had the top half of a minnow bucket, with live minnows squirming around. He had a fish stringer tied securely to his belt, his cane pole over his shoulder and an old straw hat sitting square on his head. He was a sight to behold. Then he yelled at me to get a move on and nodded to the place we were to fish.

"I was taken aback! The spot he had indicated was a long run of fast flowing water with reeds lining both sides. It appeared to be deep, but Dad assured me it was only hip-deep; on him it probably was. The bottom was smooth and free of holes and Dad probably figured there were some bass lying in the reeds. They liked to fin in the fast water and wait for something to drift by, preferably an injured minnow. Dad intended to give the bass that "something" and he waded right in, pants and all. I was a mite scared of the swift water so I lingered behind until Dad had begun to fish. I had never learned how to wade in a river. It took a certain technique, just like using that long cane pole. I wish I had a cane pole so I could demonstrate."

I told him to get on with it and forget the lecture.

"O.K., O.K!" he said, somewhat abashed. "Well, soon after Dad began fishing with that peculiar technique of his. Oh, I forgot, you don't want a lecture…"

I smiled and shrugged. I told him to go on. I was getting hungry.

"Anyway, I heard a familiar 'huh!' and there was Dad with a fish on! That settled it for me. I waded cautiously in, with my minnow bucket floating ahead of me, until the water came up to my chest. Then it leveled off and I felt more confident. Can you picture that? A small boy wading chest deep in fast water trying to keep his balance and imitate his Dad's technique of fishing with a cane pole? As I look back on it, it was a real job. It was a happy job, though, and one of the more challenging things of the afternoon. It was hard enough just to stay on my feet, let alone catch bass. Anyway, it wasn't long

FISHING WITH DAD

before I had a fish on my line, too. And that was just the beginning. Every time I threw a minnow out there, I got a bass. It was of the most exciting afternoons of my fishing life. When it was over, we had ten bass between us. It makes my fishin' fever go up just to think about it. When we held our stringers up, he on his side of the river and be on mine, the count was exactly even; five for him and five for me. If I counted the several I'd snagged but lost, I'd say I caught more than that. Dad congratulated me and allowed what a fine fisherman I turned out to be. All I could do was stand there grinning like an ape. Finally, I held my stringer up high and admitted it to be a great catch. While I was still admiring my fish, Dad waded over and relieved me of them. He told me he would stash them somewhere he thought would be safe, for me not to worry and he would be up shortly. So I untied the top half of my minnow bucket and crawled up the bank. I was itching to build my fire anyway - log cabin style, I mean - so I didn't waste any time going to work on it.

"I was so engrossed in the building of my fire that I didn't hear Dad coming. I was surprised that he had been watching me for some time. When I considered the amount of leaves and twigs to be enough

I tried to light the fire. All the leaves and twigs caught fire allright but the carefully selected short pieces of wood didn't. No matter how many times I tried it, the dadgummed wood wouldn't burn.

"Then Dad came over and kicked the whole thing down! He said, 'O.K., boy, you've tried it your way now let me try it.' The way he did it upset me so that I nearly cried. But I held on. I reckon Dad thought he would teach me a lesson on how to get over my high flying ways and learn the simple way to make a fire.

"Anyway, I guess Dad was just waiting for me to give up. He crumpled up a large piece of paper, laid it down, kicked some wood on top of it, struck a match and bingo! He had a fire going in about two minutes. A few more larger sticks and the fire began warming and drying us as a fire should. Dad said it was all very well to know how to build a fire when there was no paper around, but if there was some a person would be a fool not to use it.

"I recall him saying to me, 'Son, always use what you have.' I've always remembered that piece of advice."

The old man seemed to be finished. "Very commendable advice," I mumbled.

The Boy Scouts were packing up to leave. The old man stared emptily at them and didn't seem to hear me. He glanced at the sky, squinted his eyes and said, "We'd best be going on home."

So we did.

Years later, Dad demonstrated that he had learned well. In a downpour and with no dry wood or paper, he built a fire using gasoline soaked rags. That time he really "used what he had."

########

CHAPTER SEVENTEEN

JUST PASSING THROUGH

When you have lived in a place for a while and then moved away, going back can sometimes be a poignant experience. It was that way for me once after a long drive on a rainy night back when I was twelve.

The experience of living in a place is the total of all of the small things of daily life. In Columbia, Missouri, on Sunset Lane when I was six it meant the yellow and green breakfast nook, sunny and comfortable with corn flakes and peaches and everything peaceful. It meant playing in the sand box with the neighbor kids, looking forward to lunch. It meant listening to the radio on dark nights when Arch Obler's "Lights Out" would create a fantasy world that a little kid could half-believe. Even going to bed was a pleasurable experience because Mom would let me read before I went to sleep. Mom knew how to make bed time a positive experience. And living in a tight wooden house meant that even on stormy nights when the rain was slashing at the windows and lightning flashed I could put the pillow over my head and feel safe even when the thunder boomed.

On late summer evenings there were the strident but somehow melodic sounds of locusts (Cicadas) rising and falling on the warm, heavy air. The sounds of the big iridescent locusts were peculiarly moving. I think it was because they always ended their song on a minor note. And if the locusts were not singing sad songs the Mourning Doves were. Their plaintive cooing made me nostalgic, although at the age of six I didn't know what that was.

Later we lived in a little brick house on Delaware Street in Springfield, Missouri. I was seven. It was here where I passed that "endless summer," when I actually lost track of time. It was a genuine shock to me when September rolled around and I found that school was starting again. That was the year when there was a blizzard before Thanksgiving and our car broke down in the snow on the way to Grandma's in Joplin. After those experiences, I figured life had little more to offer me. I felt that I had done it all. That Christmas I got my first train. It was supposed to be an electric train, but I had gotten into it before Christmas. To punish me, Dad took the train set back. He bought me a wind-up train instead. I thought it was terrific. I was so happy I asked Dad if this was the set he had taken back.

"No, it's not," he said with a pained look. Dad had meant to teach me a lesson but he had only deprived himself. I didn't know the difference.

Now it was ten years later and Mom, Dad, Jerry and I were driving from Fayette to Joplin through Springfield. The day's drive had been pleasant, but as night came on and black clouds gathered I wished that we were going home rather than staying on the road.

We got into Springfield about 6 o'clock and Dad turned into a restaurant for dinner. It was the local Greyhound station. We had a nice Ozark dinner, probably chicken fried steak or a hot roast beef sandwich with gravy. Normally after such a dinner it would have been time to relax, to listen to the radio or read. But we had to go on. Outside it had started to rain. The thunder was growling and elongated. It was like the grumbling of a sleepy monster. Lightning flashed between the clouds, illuminating the wet parking lot.

Dad had a cigarette and Jerry and I had ice cream and after that it was time to leave. Supposedly we had our second wind. It was the lady at the cash register who did it to me. Dad was paying the bill while I picked up a comic book and a couple of candy bars.

"Going home and read in bed, are you?" she asked me. "Good night for it." She indicated the rain splattering the windows.

"Not tonight I'm afraid," Dad smiled. "Got to hit the road."

Then all I could think of was the warm little house on Delaware Street where I could read in bed on a rainy night and snuggle under the covers. It was only a few miles away in this very town, but the way things were it was a whole world away.

"Yep," I told the cashier, "We used to live here, but tonight we're just passing through."

Now I realize that we are just passing through life on a journey whose destination is unknown. That night we got back in our '36 Chevy and drove down the wet, dark road to Joplin. There an old man was reaching the end of his journey. Before he left he took my hand and said, "Son, will you carry on the record?"

"Yes, Grandfather, I will," I said, but I had no idea what he meant.

########

CHAPTER EIGHTEEN

CITY FISHIN'

When Dad sold the '36 Chevy during the war there was one thing he didn't consider. Without a car we couldn't go fishing.

The war was coming for me and I had a girl friend who was unfaithful. I was a gangling 17 year old growing up too fast. Daddy worked all week in Kansas City and rode the train back on week-ends. Mother ordered groceries from the store down on the square and they delivered them in boxes. Peanut butter came in a cardboard carton scooped from a bulk container. Mother kept it in our Gruno electric refrigerator. It was 1944.

"Don't worry, we'll go fishing down on the old lake if we have to take a bus," Dad had said. But it was one of those times when none of us had any hopes, only fears. We were waiting for the war to be over. If it didn't end soon, I was going to have to go. Jerry had just passed puberty and was not thrilled by the prospects. Mother was still nursing at the old hospital but she had come down with some debility for which she was taking "grass" pills. Dad would rather have been teaching but he had just been thrown out of the local college. The new Dean was not enlightened enough to accept Sociology and Family Planning as legitimate courses. Dad was back in the Government service working for the Bureau of Labor Statistics. He was denied a Navy commission. The only person in the family who was still innocent and optimistic was Mike. He was three at the time. Mike lived in a different world from the rest of us.

Dad knew that we'd feel better if we went fishing down at our old stomping grounds on the Lake of the Ozarks. But I thought even that was out because with no car how would we ever get to the lake?

"Next week-end," Dad said, "We'll get all of our stuff together and go down to the bus station."

"I can't believe it," I said. "We're going fishing on a bus?"

"I guess it's been done before," Dad said.

So that started it. For a week we went through our equipment and picked out what we would take. We broke our rods down and tied them together. We took only one tackle box with the bare necessities like reels, lures, hooks and a stringer. No minnow bucket or net, no extra rods and none of the amenities like bug repellant, sun tan lotion or even big bobbers. Almost fifty years later I would remember all this when I had to carry all of my equipment on an airplane to get to the same lake.

But in 1944 it was the first time we had to take public transportation to go fishing. I couldn't imagine how we'd get to our cabin. Would we have to walk for miles from the highway down those old rocky roads in the woods?

Dad gave us the word. "Don't expect this to be one of our normal fishing trips. We'll get a place close to the highway and close to the lake. There's a place right above low bridge I was thinking of. They rent cabins and boats. That's all we need. We'll have to change busses in Jeff City and go south from there. Don't pack too many clothes."

Dad called a cab to go to the bus station. At least I wouldn't have to carry our fishing tackle down the main street in front of everybody! Mom and Mike weren't going, so we all waved goodbye feeling funny about the whole thing.

"Everything has to be portable. After we get there and settle in you can pretend the old '36 Chevy is right outside. But we can't change base."

"Just getting back to the old lake will be great," I said and poked Jerry. But Jerry was kind of morose. He seemed to be taking it personally that we had no car.

We didn't know when we were kids how independent a car made us. We found many an old fishing camp at the end of a washed out rocky road. Often we had camped out right by the car, using it as an anchor. And when Dad wanted to change base from one arm of the lake to another, we just drove away.

"Why don't we have our car anymore?" Jerry asked.

"It's the war, kid," Dad said. "There's not much gasoline and you can't even buy tires. They won't even give me a car at work."

"But that was our car," Jerry grumped. "Nobody could take it away from you just because of the old war."

"No, but it would have just sat there not being used and falling apart."

"Now somebody else has it."

"I suppose..." Dad looked sad too.

"Don't worry, we'll get another car after the war," I said.

"Yeah," Jerry said. "If you come back."

It was the first time Jerry had expressed any concern at all about what might happen to me. I felt an unfamiliar surge of feeling for the kid. But all I said was, "Hey!" Jerry smiled.

If you're an old timer, you've probably ridden on lots of cross-crountry busses. Greyhound was a national institution in the 1940's and '50's. Our bus that day was a local from Fayette to Jeff City. We got aboard and stuffed our fishing equipment and luggage into the overhead racks. Some people looked at us peculiarly. But we just looked secretive and sat down for the ride. Two hours later we were at the bus station in Jeff City. "We have a half hour lay-over, boys," Dad announced, "so we might as well have a Coke or something." Coca Cola was a nickle and came in 6-ounce green bottles from a machine. A Pepsi Cola sign announced, "Pepsi Cola hits the spot! Twelve full ounces, that's a lot. Twice as much for a nickle, too! Pepsi Cola is the drink for you!" Most people preferred "Coke" anyway. R.C Cola and Nehi were in coolers. Jerry had a grape Nehi. Dad and I had Cokes.

I sat there thinking about my perfidious girlfriend who had gone back home that summer for a visit and was promptly seduced by her cousin. It could have been the other way around. The juke box was blaring Harry James with his new hit, "It Seems To Me I've Heard That Song Before." Four years later she married the guy so I guess it was all right. But right then I was plenty miserable.

"Board!" the bus driver called. "Eldon, Lake Ozark, Osage Beach and Camdenton." That was our country and I felt like we were going home.

Dad was right. The bus let us off just across the bridge and all we had to do was walk up the hill to the resort. It was a little fancier than we were used to because it was right on the highway. But back up on the hill there were some old fashioned cabins and we moved into one right away.

"Look," Jerry said, "It has a kerosine stove."

"Right," Dad said, "and a couple of bunks and a sink to clean our fish on."

"Beats sleeping on the ground," I said.

"I don't know, let's take a look outside."

"No bedding or ground cloth," I reminded Dad. "We're city fishin' this time. We can't take any fish back, either. No cooler, no ice and no minnow bucket."

When we got down to the dock that afternoon there were two wooden boats left with no motors. We took one of them and went out on the lake. But there wasn't much natural cover at this location, right before Low Bridge and with cabins and resorts all along the shore. The lake was pretty wide at this point, too, and big cabin cruisers were tooling up and down like they owned it.

But we rowed around and did some fishing anyhow. We cast around the docks and out in the deep water. We got no strikes. We fished around under the bridge, hearing the roar and rattle of traffic overhead. Then the wind came up and we decided to pack it in for that day. We all felt cheated because we couldn't fish in a decent spot. But nobody said anything because we had agreed to the circumstances.

I remember all of this because it turned out that this was the last time we would fish on the Lake of the Ozarks. Shortly after I enlisted in the Navy, the folks moved to Dallas where Dad had a job at S.M.U. Both Jerry and Mike grew up in Dallas and after the war I went there too. Come to think of it, Daddy may never have fished the Lake of the Ozarks again after that summer bus trip. I didn't get back to it myself for almost 50 years! But we didn't know that then.

The next morning the papers were full of a deep dark tragedy. The Missouri Highway Patrol had fished a body out of the lake right there at Low Bridge! And the body had no head! "I guess we'd better be careful what we catch today," I said.

"Why?" Jerry asked innocently.

"Because we might hook that...head," I said.

"Oh, no!" Jerry moaned. "I'm not going out there."

"Don't worry," Dad said. "All we're going to do today is drown some worms. There ought to be some action under that bridge."

Jerry looked uncertain and I felt a little funny too. That's just where they had found the body. The rest of it might be hanging around. The thought of it gave me goosebumps. "What's the matter?" Jerry asked.

"Oh nothing. I just got a little sunburn yesterday," I told him. Dad laughed.

So we spent another day "city fishin'" like all of the common folks, waiting for something to come by and nip our worms. It wasn't the kind of fishing we liked but at least we were fishing. I caught three perch and a crappie that day and Dad and Jerry caught a few too. They were the kind of fish that you throw back after happily wiping slime and scales on your pants. We had taken the boat so we could tie up at various points under the bridge. Every time we moved, Jerry looked suspiciously at the dark water. He was thinking about that head. And with all of the heavy traffic on the bridge and the unfamiliar type of fishing we were doing plus the uncertainty of the times, we soon took the boat back in. "We'll cast along the docks again this evening," Dad said.

After the heat of the day wore off and the sun was somewhere west of Warsaw we got back into the old wooden boat. "You take the oars, son," Dad told me, "so I can get some casting done." It was just like old times except that I was a little better at rowing than when I was Jerry's age. I pulled away from the resort dock and headed away from the bridge. It was odd because now instead of putting Daddy close to logs and brush in a cove I was just getting him close to another dock. "Sometimes bass feed around docks for the little feesh," Dad said, and heaved a good one on his old casting reel. The plug plopped in the right place and lay there twitching. KERBLAM! Dad had a fish! "Oh, boy!" Dad said. After two days of hand-sized blue gill, Dad had lit into what seemed to be a fairly big bass. Anyhow the bass took off for the dock and ran around all the pilings. But Dad kept enough pressure on to keep the bass from tangling him up. After about five minutes of tussle the bass was free of the dock and coming toward the boat. I could tell it was a big smallmouth because he fought harder as Dad brought him closer to the boat.

"Get out the net!"

"No net."

"Rig the stringer."

"No stringer."

"Maybe you got a pot!"

"What?"

"To piss in!"

"Don't have that, either," I laughed. Jerry looked puzzled.

"Bring him around here," Jerry said at the front of the boat, "I'll get him."

It turned out to be about a 3-pound smallmouth, as pretty a fish as you'd ever see. I could see the anguish written on Dad's face as he thought about letting him go. "Just let him flop around on the floor, Dad," I said. "We'll take him back and have him for supper. Maybe you'll get another one."

Dad smiled. "O.K., Jerry, it's your job to see that he doesn't flop out of the boat."

Jerry looked worried, but he stuck the fish under the duck boards on the bottom of the boat and kept an eye on him.

Meanwhile, Dad had his plug back in the water. I pulled him quietly from one dock to another but there was no more action. It was getting dark. Yellow lights were beginnning to appear in the windows of cabins on the hill. I heard a screen door slam and somebody yelling for their kids. A dog barked somewhere. An evening breeze came up and ruffled the dark water. I pulled for home.

Tomorrow we had to get back on the bus. But tonight it would be like we were just packing up to get in the old car and change our base. Dad cleaned his bass and cooked it up with scrambled eggs and fried potatoes. We would each have some of the bass along with toast and milk and other good things. Dad had actually bought an apple pie with cheese for dessert. The kerosine stove wafted nostalgic fumes through the cabin along with the delicate aromas of frying fish and potatoes. We had a great supper and cleaned up every bit of it.

"Remember how we used to fish down at Twin Bays and stay in those cabins with the tin roofs?" I said.

Dad grunted. "Jerry probably remembers Twin Bays more for the mosquitoes than anything else."

"Out on the island," Jerry said.

"I remember all those silver bass!" I said.

"You caught your first fish down by the camp on the Gravois, remember?" Dad asked.

"Yeah," I said. "I hope it won't be my last."

Jerry laughed. "While you're gone I'm going to learn how to cast like Dad and catch all of the bass."

It was kind of quiet after that because that led to all sorts of thoughts. How would I ever get through boot camp? How would I ever survive being at sea and getting blown out of the water? Why didn't they end the war? When would I ever sit in a cabin like this again eating apple pie and cheese with my Dad and brother?

Outside the katydids started up and they were joined by all sorts of tree frogs and crickets. It was a summer night symphony in the Missouri woods. The night sounds were so loud you'd wonder how anybody got any sleep. But for us those sounds were as comforting as a lullaby. Sometimes I could understand why Dad liked to sleep outdoors.

About that time a big diesel truck went by on the highway not far away, blaring its horn and shattering the illusion.

"Better get some sleep, boys," Dad said. "Tomorrow it's back to the city."

########

CHAPTER NINETEEN

THE ROAD TO THOMASVILLE

Shortly after Jerry and Dad had perfected their "escape" routine of driving back to the Ozarks from Texas, I moved back to Dallas and was invited to go along. When Dad asked me if I wanted to go fishing I thought he meant to Possum Kingdom or Lake Dallas.

"No," Dad said, "I mean a real fishin' trip, back where you haven't been in a long time!"

"Sounds great. Where?" I asked.

"Thomasville. Going to go fishin' on Eleven Point."

So Dad was trying to capture his past again. Jerry was bright-eyed because he was looking forward to smoking more cigars and blazing up the highway in Dad's new post-war car, a 1948 Chrysler. As for me, I had never been to Thomasville before except in my mother's womb.

FISHING WITH DAD

Jerry and I had done a lot of fishing with Dad, but this was going to be different. We were all grown now. I had been to the wars and back again and Jerry was almost graduated. Dad was a full professor at S.M.U.

At first it was Dad who drove. It was his escape after all and we were just the kids. He put his foot down and the Chrysler roared off. North Texas highways were flat and straight and if the car had had wings, Dad would have been at 10-thousand feet.

In those days, Oklahoma roads were a different story. There was no turnpike and all of the main roads were torture racks - narrow and full of holes. This gave Jerry and me more time to stamp white horses, a game we had played as kids. I sat in front because I was the oldest. Dad "shot down" the cars that we passed. It was just like when we were kids and that was part of the escape. The only thing that was different was the amount of whiskey Dad drank. At that time, I thought it was good that he was relaxing.

It got dark and Dad drove on. I dozed and Jerry slept on the back seat.

We arrived in Vinita, Oklahoma, about 3:30 A.M. Dad drove down the main street, with its Western style false fronted buildings, and pulled up in front of a diner. He turned around in his seat and poked Jerry. "We're here, kid," he said. Jerry just groaned. Dad looked at me and said, "Let's go in for coffee and see if Pic has been around." I opened Jerry's door and when the arm rest was pulled out from under his head, he finally woke up. Pic "Doc" Darrough was our Uncle - our mother's sister's husband. He was Chief Surgeon at the hospital and he worked a lot at night. Pic's office was in the neighborhood and late at night he would sometimes come by that diner. I remember Dad told us he once met Pic there about 4 A.M..

But this morning, Pic wasn't there. We walked in and Dad, half-asleep, made a remark about "getting a drink" in there. The all-night cook looked puzzled, not realizing it was Dad's little joke. Oklahoma was then a dry state.

"Has Doc Darrough been in tonight?" Dad asked.

"Nah," the cook answered, "Not tonight. Big wreck out on the highway and he's been busy." We looked at each other and sipped our coffee.

"Well if you see him tell him his brother was by tonight," Dad said. "He'll know who it is."

"You Doc's brother?" the cook looked more closely at Dad. "Nice to know you!" Everyone in Vinita had great respect for Pic Darrough. He was quite a man. Pic's father had been a U.S. Marshal when Oklahoma was first a state. Pic drove cattle, rode bulls and was a crack shot. He was also a whiz of a doctor.

"I'm Doc's brother-in-law," Dad said, "and these are his nephews. Come on boys, dawn's a-breakin'."

It was Jerry's turn to drive and Dad curled up in the back seat and went to sleep. I took my place in the navigator's seat. "Let's go, kid," I mimicked Dad. Jerry smirked and the Chrysler roared off.

At 4 A.M. the road northeast out of Vinita was a dark and mysterious path. Any road on the Oklahoma plains at that time of the morning was eerie. We were in a warm, throbbing cocoon with lights and a radio. Outside, dark little farms went by and the road took sudden turns. One of the odd things about driving at night is that you can hear crickets and other night creatures singing, even though you are streaking past them at 60 miles an hour. Jerry gripped the wheel grimly while I just dozed off and left the world to him.

The next thing I knew the sky was light and the Chrysler was slowing down. The "sandpiles" of Joplin, old zinc tailings, flashed past the window. Jerry had passed the city limits. In a few minutes, we were driving downtown. Dad sat up in the back seat, blinked his eyes and saw he was in his old home town.

"Good Lord," he said, "I can't believe I'm on Main Street in Joplin." He had already gone back to the past. Back "up that-a-way" on North Joplin Street was where Dad had grown up. His father's grocery store, "The Pearl", had been on Main Street. Naturally, Dad had many more memories of the place than I did. But I had a few, too. I had been born there.

I couldn't help sensing that Dad was not just feeling nostalgic about the place. He was also rejecting his present life as a responsible college Professor, with all of its attendant stress, and his socially-conscious wife who had pushed him all their married life to become a more important person. And now Daddy was more important. But he didn't like it much. By that time I was over 21 and, unlike Dad, not being pushed at all to become more important. In fact, I was staring at total failure and an uncertain future. Unlike Dad, I didn't want to be a "hillbilly" and spend my life in the woods. Mother always said I was "cut out for better things" but I didn't know what that meant. At least Dad knew what he really wanted to do, even if he couldn't do it.

I knew what I liked doing which was writing radio shows and doing audio production but I was ahead of my time and could not make any money at it then.

We spent the night on a back road someplace south of Willow Springs. The next morning, the Chrysler broke a leaf spring while we were trying to get back on the main road and we limped into West Plains to get it fixed. Thomasville, only about 25 miles away, would have to wait until that afternoon.

########

CHAPTER TWENTY

FISHING ON ELEVEN POINT

I thought I was prepared for our entry into Thomasville that May afternoon in 1948, but nobody had told me that it would look like it did in 1926! I'm sure that there had been some improvements which I didn't notice, such as indoor plumbing and electricity but when I first saw the place it was as if an old picture had come to life. I looked around and thought, "this can't be where Daddy had wanted us to live!"

"It used to be a lot bigger," Dad said. I laughed. Jerry looked puzzled. "They must have torn down some of the houses. Maybe there was a fire. Where are all the outhouses?" I looked down the dusty main street and it seemed like every other lot was empty. "I see the old store is still there though," Dad said and drove the Chrysler up in front of an old stone building with a tin roof. There was a soft drink cooler in front.

FISHING WITH DAD

We had descended from a rolling road that afternoon after spending all morning in the garage in West Plains. The Chrysler's broken spring had taken hours to fix and then finally we were off to Thomasville.

Dad probably remembered the days when it took hours to get to Thomasville from West Plains in his Model "T" so he wasn't much bothered. The road was rolling, narrow and dusty. It dipped to go across creeks and rose in roller coaster fashion up the opposite bank.

We clattered across the narrow bridge over the Eleven Point river and into town at about 11 o'clock. Thomasville was strangely quiet at that time of day and seemed to be dozing in the sun. There were three older men sitting by the drink cooler when we drove up. They looked at us suspiciously as if we were invading their territory, which I suppose we were. Dad said "Howdy" to the men as we hauled out of the car. We wanted something cold to drink. Dad and I dragged out ice cold beers and Jerry found a grape Nehi. One of the old men asked if I was of age.

"I'm 21," I said, not telling him I was also a World War Two veteran, married and out of work.

"He's 21, all right," Dad said. "And I ought to know since I'm his Daddy." They all looked at me while Dad grinned. It must have been some old Ozark joke. I think Dad thought he knew those men from when he had lived there 22 years before.

After passing a few astute remarks like, "it looks like rain" and "lots of skeeters this year", we went into the store.

It was a real general store with everything from tires to whiskey. Dad bought a bottle of bourbon for himself and a box of crackers for the minnow trap.

When we walked out of the store, the old men nodded and Dad asked about various houses and what had happened to them. This was to let them know that he had lived there once and he knew their town. Occasionally they would glance sideways at me. They were probably thinking, "so that's the kid who would have grown up here if Mac's wife had let him."

Looking at the old men in their overalls, then looking at Dad, I shook my head. Even though Dad was trying to fit in the contrast was remarkable.

Dad was a full professor at S.M.U. and, despite his rumpled fishing clothes, his dignity and position showed through. The men to whom Dad was talking were about his age but they looked much older. They wore faded overalls and heavy shoes. I didn't really know who they were but it occurred to me that if Dad had stayed here he would probably look like they did. That was unthinkable. Mother was right to make Dad leave.

But maybe I should not have been so critical. These men had good, clean, simple lives. They had everything arranged just like they wanted and had no thoughts or cares about the sort of life from which Dad was trying to escape.

As for me, had I grown up in Thomasville I would probably have had a simpler life. Fewer choices would have meant fewer mistakes. I looked out over the town, but I didn't see much activity. I heard some children playing somewhere but I saw no young people. Perhaps they had all left town like Dad had.

I felt strangely uncomfortable as Dad asked more questions and the men waved toward the river.

I was remembering when I had lived in the Ozarks before. I went through the 6th grade in short pants while my peers wore overalls. I didn't get into many fights but I had to do a lot of quick thinking to stay out of them. To my Ozark classmates I was a snobby city boy. To me they were a little fearsome. Although the country kids had limited experience compared to me they were all bigger than I was and their responses were more physical. I never did fit in, but I didn't have to. In a year we were off to Columbia and another career.

But that was long ago, and now I was looking at my roots and wondering if I would have made a good Ozark kid. We started saying our goodbyes and Dad told the men that we were going to camp out by the old bridge and do a little fishing. We hopped into the car and drove down the main street. I looked at the houses as we passed, wondering, "was this where Mom and Dad lived?" But Dad was looking for the road to the bridge.

He found the turn and soon we were back on the river. We clattered across the old bridge, then took a left across the road to a wide spot close to the river. Eleven Point gurgled happily not far away. It was beautiful and busy and I could see why Dad liked it. We stumbled down the rocky bank to the river. At this point there was a wide bed of gravel and sand of which the river was using only about 20-feet. It was a perfect place for a temporary camp.

As usual Dad picked the site, staked it out, put the minnow trap in the water and built a rock fireplace. And as usual, Jerry had built a fire after I had gathered the drift wood and sticks. Neither one of them ever asked me to do anything else. From my point of view, I felt useless but fortunate to have them along for survival. From their point of view, I probably just appeared to be lazy. If someone else would do a job, I would let them. It was good training for when I grew older and became the senior member, or Patriarch, of camping and fishing groups. Nowadays nobody expects me to do anything, although with my vast experience they know that I could do it all if I wanted to!

Anyway, there we were on the bank of the fabled Eleven Point River, the water fast and cold and the day waning. Daddy didn't seem to be in any hurry to put rods together. He seemed distant and enthralled.

Dad sat on the sand with his back against a log and drank from his bottle. Jerry busied himself unrolling bedding and squaring away the camp. We had no tents this time, just tarps, blankets and a ground cloth. Dad roused himself to make dinner, and we sat around quietly eating and thinking our own thoughts.

"All right, boys," Dad said suddenly. "Let's give a cheer for the old river!" All three of us let go with our own versions of the Rebel Yell. We looked at Dad in expectation of his next move but after our sudden yelling, he just slumped down. The wet warbling of the river became the only sound.

The campfire died down. The night grew darker. We all crawled into our bedding and I grew drowsy. It was a wonderful place to sleep. Then Dad got up on his elbow.

"When I was a kid here I used to talk your mother into sleeping out on the bank like this. She didn't like it much, but we were just married and I was usually able to distract her." He smiled at us. We looked at him in horror. We didn't want to hear about their love-life! Daddy looked away, rustled around in his bag for his bottle, sort of saluted the river with it and took a last drink. "Goodnight boys," he said, rather quietly.

Dad's sentimental journey back to Thomasville had stirred up emotions in him that he hadn't expected. We had never seen Dad go soft. His role as our father had been one of a tough macho man, sensible and humorous yet very strict. He was one great guy with no weaknesses who had all the answers. The idea that Dad had a different personality from the one he had always shown to us was kind of frightening.

It started raining during the night and I woke up with my bedding pulled up over my head. It was dawn now and time to get up and go fishin'! We were lying right by the river and all we had to do was roll over and start casting. But somehow that wet and foggy morning getting up and lurching into the cold river was the last thing I wanted to do!

I peeled back my rain cover and squinted at the dawn. It was still drizzling and a mist rose from the river. I looked over and saw that Jerry was a lump. Even Dad was totally covered. Then I seized the moment! It was my big chance to pull one on them. I wiggled out of my bag, grabbed a rod, put it together and started yelling. "Wahoo! I got one! I got a big one!" I kicked Jerry's bag. He just grunted. "Come on, boys!" I hollered, "Time to go fishin'!"

Dad whipped off his head cover. "What the hell?" he said groggily.

I stood there waving the rod and smiling stupidly. Jerry rolled over. Dad took a quick look around, eyed me like I was crazy, and pulled the cover back over his head. That was it. I could tell they didn't want to go fishing. I was getting cold and wet and the fireplace was a soggy mess. I hoped that they wouldn't expect me to start the fire. So I went back to bed and I lay there listening to the river.

Nothing happened for about an hour. Then I heard Dad kick off his bedroll. I sat up and saw him go down to the minnow trap. He lifted the trap and it was full of big chub minnows.

"Looks like this is all we're going to catch today," Dad said. He still seemed far away somewhere. Jerry sat up, too. I wondered who would start the fire. Then down at the river I saw Dad open the minnow trap and dump all the silver chub minnows back into the water. "Go on home, guys. Your mother's waiting."

He smiled up at us, then took a long, last look at his beloved Eleven Point. "It's mighty pretty," I heard him say, "but it's got a cold heart." Then he looked back to where we were standing. "Come on boys, let's go find us a good breakfast somewhere."

So we were going to leave the river bank, load up and drive off without wetting a line. There might have been more than one reason for this. First, it wasn't going to be a good fishing day. Then the wet bones of last night's fire looked pretty hopeless. And the river itself was low with few pools or submerged riffles in which to fish.

But I always thought there was another reason we didn't stay that day. Dad didn't seem to want to fish his Eleven Point River again. Although it was the symbol of his lost youth and he had caught many a string of fish there, Dad was now a long way from those carefree days. He was another person with another life. And even though he didn't like it much he had to admit that the old saying might be true:

"You can't go home again."

But you can try.

########

CHAPTER TWENTY-ONE

BIG SPRING

Great Grandfather Granville must have been a prodigious wet weather camper. Four years in the Union Army from 1861 to 1865 taught him every trick in the book of wet camp survival. His death certificate said that he died, at age 58, of a number of service-related ailments he caught in army camps and in the Confederate prison at Andersonville, Georgia. He probably spent a third of his one thousand, four hundred and sixty nights in the army on wet ground. He also spent about 6 months on the ground or in a hole at Andersonville.

One would think that after all of that he would never in his life ever want to sleep on the ground again! But as sometimes happens, after 20 years or so in the old feather bed Granville began to look back on all of his suffering with a touch of nostalgia.

When he later took his children out into the woods to show them the wonders of nature he proudly passed on to them all of his wet camp techniques. He showed his boys, John and Lee, how to drain the ground around a tent, how to dig a latrine, how to make a fire out of wet wood, how to sleep warm and dry in muddy water and even how to keep warm in a wet blanket. He also could have taught them how to keep gunpowder dry in a rainstorm and how to elude an enemy in the forest but fortunately they never needed those skills.

So Great Grandfather Granville's experience was the basis of three generations of wet camp freaks who were as at home in the dripping wilderness as the rest of us are in a warm, dry cabin.

It was always comforting to me to know that both my brother and my Dad were skilled and experienced campers with all of the knowledge necessary to survive in the wilderness. All I ever had to do was just watch them and take orders.

The week-end when we traveled back to Thomasville was no different. On the way back from our night on the gravel bar on Eleven Point, we drove east and then south on a back road where Dad and his Dad before him had camped in the wilderness. Dad kept saying how things had changed. There was even a sign to the spring on a new graveled road. Dad took the road, muttering that he and his Dad had walked in to it, busting brush and blazing a trail.

Meanwhile, it had started to rain. "It's just a drizzle," Dad said and wouldn't turn on the wipers. The road got a little bumpy. Some of the holes were full of water. "This is more like it," he said, wrestling with the steering wheel. Suddenly we were there, at a wide spot in the road with loud water noises coming from ahead. Dad drove under a tree and killed the engine.

We piled out to take a look at the spring. It boiled out of a crack in the granite and spilled with great force into a wide and deep pool at our feet. It must have been a hundred feet across and no telling how deep. At the other end of the pool the water roared off into a wild stream that emptied into a river somewhere. Dad smiled and went to get his tackle. Meanwhile, Jerry and I broke out our fishing gear and proceeded to cast into the cold, deep, roiling pool.

It kept drizzling and we had our hats pulled down while we cast our lures into the good-looking water. But no matter what we threw in, we got no strikes. It was good exercise but not much else.

FISHING WITH DAD

Dad went down to where the angry little creek splashed and gurgled. He fished a few holes and gave up. But he seemed happy, as if just going through the motions here at the old spring where he had fished with his Dad was enough. He looked at the whole area as a kind of shrine. I have no idea if he had ever caught anything there.

"Might as well set up camp, seeing as how it's getting darker and wetter."

I could tell that Dad didn't want to build a fire and cook anything, so we settled for cold rations that night. We sat in the car as the rain grew harder and made a mess with sardines, crackers and cheese.

"Why don't we just sleep in the car?" I asked.

"What, and sit up all night? Nah," Dad said, "We got a ground cloth and a tarp. I can keep dry in that. One of you can sleep in the car."

I looked at Jerry but he was already busy stringing one of the tarps up as a shelter. He tied two corners to tree branches and secured the other side to the car by slipping the canvas through the windows and rolling them up. That didn't work too well, so he just slammed the doors on the canvas and that kept it tight. Dad put his ground cloth down, blankets on top of that, then rolled up in the whole thing. We didn't use sleeping bags.

So it was out in the rain for the wet camp freaks to get some sleep. Fortunately for me, there were no more tarps and I had to sacrifice and sleep in the back seat of the car. Dad and Jerry did not act like they were suffering or envious of my warm, dry bed. They seemed to enjoy the wet, miserable night. I knew that I should be sorry for the poor guys but I was not about to give up the back seat. Besides, somebody could have slept in the front seat. Jerry was just being stubborn.

I liked the sound of the rain on the car's roof and I put out of my mind the misery my brother and father might be going through. Fact is, they were probably enjoying it, dreaming of the days when Great Grandfather Granville had slept like this many a night on long marches through Georgia.

The night ended with a great thunder crash. The trees were still dripping and it was overcast but the rain had stopped. I sat up and looked out the car window. Dad was a dark lump under a leafy bough that hung almost to the ground. Jerry was sleeping almost under the car. The tarp he had hung above him to keep the rain off was bulging down! Because there was no slope to the tarp the rain had pooled in a low spot. The weight of the water had pulled the tree branches lower and made room for an even bigger pool. By this time, the tarp was almost half full of water and hanging only inches above Jerry's head!

Jerry was still quiet but I knew that the minute he touched the tarp it would explode on him. I slowly lowered the rear car door window.

"Jerry!" I called softly.

"Mnphh?"

"Get up, Jerry, the tarp is full of water." Jerry moved, turned on his back and saw what was hanging over him. He hissed. "Wait a minute," I said, "I'll come out and help you." Then I stupidly opened the car door!

What happened next is a classic in the annals of wet camping. Jerry just lay there while tons of cold water splashed down on him. I tried to grab the tarp as it let go but it was too late. Jerry leaped up, and was immediately surrounded by the wet tarp. He threw everything off of him and turned to glare at me.

"What the hell?" I heard Dad ask.

Then Jerry started laughing. "Might as well open the other door so it can all fall down," he said. When he said this I stepped out into the mud to open the other door and my warm, dry body fell flat into the cold, slimy ooze. That really made Jerry laugh and he started dancing around. With his blankets and tarp wrapped around him, he looked like the Indian that he was. I suppose I got what I deserved.

The rain held off until we got ourselves straightened out. Dad was the only one who acted like he had had a good night's sleep in a warm bed. We piled into the car, shivering and still asleep. Dad looked at us both and started the car.

"What say we go find ourselves an Ozark breakfast somewhere up the road?"

"Sounds good to me, Dad. Any place that's dry!" I said.

########

CHAPTER TWENTY-TWO

FISHING IN THE TREETOPS

When Dad moved the family to Dallas in the mid- 1940's, he found that Texas lakes were not anything like Missouri's. They were mostly limestone basins with hardly any tree cover, full of clear water and smallmouth bass.

If Dad couldn't fish in the Ozarks, then he fished wherever he could. He tried what he called "Texas bathtubs", but he preferred to look for lakes and fishing camps that reminded him of the Ozarks.

Possum Kingdom was one of those lakes. The lake itself, 100 miles West of Dallas on a tributary of the Brazos, was in the middle of storied Comanche country. Weatherford and Mineral Wells, both hot, dry places, were East of Possum Kingdom. It was about as far from Dallas-Fort Worth to the lake as it was further west to Abilene. Yet the North-South lake had enough reach, curves and coves to remind Dad of the Lake of the Ozarks.

Back then, the few fishing camps around the lake were the old-fashioned kind, with a smoky central lodge and a few primitive cabins, the kind with big nails in the rough walls to hang things on and one bare bulb hanging on a single wire. This suited Dad just fine. He could track mud onto the floor, bring his rods and stringer inside and sleep with his shoes on. Out in West Texas it was sometimes wiser to keep your shoes on at all times anyway.

Despite Possum Kingdom's similarities to an Ozark lake, the wildlife around there was definitely Texas-style; big and mean. The larger varmints usually kept to themselves, but it was not unknown to find some of the other creatures sharing quarters with you.

Dad, Jerry and I went to Possum Kingdom one Fall after a long, hot Texas summer. The roads were dry, the grasshoppers were thick and even the Mesquite was drooping. But after we drove through the sagging wire gate to get to the fishing camp the temperature dropped at least 10 degrees. Big Liveoaks shaded the dusty road. A south wind blew off the lake.

At the camp office we signed in and asked about the fishing. "Lake's low," the man said. He turned out to be the owner. "Getting most of 'em on minnows and worms in deep water."

We found our cabin and Daddy let out a great sigh and lay on the bed. In a minute he was sawing away, so I figured there would be no fishing that evening. Jerry and I brought in all the supplies and tackle and sat around jawing and putting things together. It was rare for the three of us to sleep in a cabin. The days of sleeping on the ground and fighting nature seemed to be over for us. Little did I know Dad's secret plan.

He sprang it on us the next morning at dawn. He went down and got a 14-foot wooden V-bottom with a 7.5 horse motor. Then he told us to start loading it, to bring the sleeping bags, the food boxes and the flashlight. I looked at Jerry and he shrugged. Pretty soon the boat looked like a Rogers Rangers canoe. We barely fit in it with all of the rods, minnow buckets and tackle boxes. Dad turned the boat around with his paddle and yanked the motor to life. Then he grinned. "Oh boy," he said.

It might have been a West Texas lake, but it sure looked like the Ozarks. For one thing it was not a limestone basin but a flooded valley. It was a rather young lake so lots of the bushes and trees were still there. We found that out as we proceeded down the lake.

Suddenly we saw a forest of tree-tops poking above water. They had not cut the trees down when they drowned the valley and the lake was low. The tallest trees were showing their tops and we headed for them.

"How tall are those trees, do you think?" I asked.

"Can't see the bottom. They might be fifty feet," Dad said. "Fish like to congregate around trees, so let's go in." Dad cut the motor and we drifted in among the tree tops. Most of them were young oaks. Some might have been black walnut. They were all dead. We just tied up to a limb and dropped our lines.

"We'll just see how deep it is," Dad said, and started unspooling line. He snubbed the line at about 45-feet, and immediately got a bite. Up came a pan-sized crappie. Meanwhile, both Jerry and I were doing the same thing. Every time the line went down, a crappie came up. Sometimes a strike was harder and the fight longer. Bass were feeding along with the crappie. We sat there for hours and pulled in two double stringers of keepers.

"Never caught fish like this before," Dad said.

"Now comes the hard part," I said, "Cleaning them!"

"You gut them, I'll scale them," Jerry said.

We had cast off from the trees and were "putting" back up the lake looking for a campsite when there was a thrashing in the water ahead of us. Dad cut the motor. I thought that a big fish had jumped and that Dad was going to cast in that direction. But the thrashing continued.

"What the hell?" Dad said. Something was splashing around on the surface. I thought it was a bird or a duck. But as we came closer, we could see fins sticking out of the water. A great struggle was going on. It turned out to be slightly unbelievable.

"Nobody's going to believe this," Dad said.

"It's a big bass!" I said.

"It's two bass!" Jerry said. Dad didn't say anything. He just paddled the boat closer and nettled the bass on the surface. The net came in dripping and we could see what had happened. A large bass, about a 5-pounder, had taken a swipe at a smaller bass, about a pound and a half, and had gotten the other fish caught in his throat! There was no way the big bass could have spit out the smaller one because of his fins.

"I told you no one would believe it," Dad said. He ripped the smaller fish out and put both bass on his stringer. "Maybe it would be best if we didn't tell anybody about this."

I could tell what was going through Dad's mind. He wanted to go camp somewhere and have a fish dinner. But we had so many fish and now this huge bass and he was thinking about all of the fish stories he could tell to hangers-on at the dock and fishing camp. There was a gleam in his eye.

"You know," he said, "We've got too many fish to clean to do it out in the woods. Besides, it might rain. Let's just head back to the cabin." He looked innocently up in the sky.

There wasn't a cloud in the sky and we were in West Texas. But Jerry and I were not about to argue. Dad started the motor and we went buzzing back to the dock.

Our stringers got the proper attention alright and by the time we were cleaning them a small crowd had gathered. We had sixteen crappie and eight bass, plus the big lunker we had netted.

"What a bass!" someone said. "How'd you get him?"

"Well now, that's a long story," Dad said.

"We got him with another bass," Jerry said.

"I guess you could say that," Dad laughed. But he wouldn't tell them how it really happened. It was enough that he was the hero of the moment. I was just happy that I wasn't going to have to sleep on the ground that night!

########

CHAPTER TWENTY-THREE

FISHING WITH JERRY

When we were kids my brother Jerry and I did a lot of fishing together, learning the art of angling from our Dad. During our childhood Jerry was taught the same as I was but he never seemed to bloom. I always caught more fish. I always recognized the best fishing holes. I always made the best casts. I always rowed the boat.

So it came as some surprise to me, ten years after we grew up, that Jerry had become a master fisherman.

He was competitive, knowledgeable, accurate and crafty.

We were out together on a lake somewhere and I was showing off the fishing skills I had learned from dad. I made a cast by a log and I thought it was pretty good.

"Here, let me try that spot," Jerry said. And he flipped his lure in there right on the money. Then he smirked a little and said, "See how it's done?"

"So, where's the fish?" I asked.

"As long as it's a good cast nobody cares if you catch anything," said Jerry.

I knew where I had heard that before - from dad!

Something had happened between the time I left home and that first fishing trip Jerry and I took together. As I have said, Jerry was always more proficient in camping skills than I. He was always more skillful at woodsmanship and survival. But as long as we lived together at home I was always the better fisherman. I learned later that after I left home Dad took Jerry on solitary fishing trips to instill in him the "Mountain Man" qualities that didn't quite take with me. And without me around to get all of the attention, Jerry absorbed all of Dad's teachings with a vengeance.

Like anybody else, Jerry loved to be a winner. But he took a special pride in winning over me. It was probably because when we were kids I made sure that I always won! It was tough to always be a loser to your big brother, especially when you could see that your big brother was sometimes cheating to get the win.

After we grew up Jerry continued the competition. As an adult I didn't need to win over my brother. But Jerry felt like he had a lot to make up for. Yet when he did win over me as an adult, it didn't seem to satisfy him. Jerry was only grimly amused by my loss and he would immediately set out to beat me again. And the battles were not always games.

When I was 18, I weighed 127 pounds. By the time I was 40, I was having trouble keeping below 200 pounds. For the first 30 years of my life I was just plain skinny, so it was almost impossible for me to think of myself as "fat."

Of course others saw my condition right away. This was especially true of Jerry, who for some perverse reason was not exceptionally skinny at 18 or especially fat at 40.

Although Jerry accepted my weight as an unlucky thing that had happened to me, he was secretly delighted that it wasn't happening to him. In fact, he was openly amused at times when my uncharacteristic weight caused a comment or a problem.

Once when I was visiting and his children were very small, one of them - I think it was Joey - asked, "Daddy, is Uncle David really your brother?"

"Why, of course, Joey." Jerry answered.

"Then why is he so fat, and you're not?"

Incidents like that amused Jerry no end and of course his amusement stemmed from his winning a battle that I was losing.

By the time Jerry and I were both middle aged I figured that all of our childhood antagonisms had been laid to rest. Little did I know that In Jerry they were lying very near the surface.

Lake Springfield was what they called a "city lake", close-by and relatively small. But when we got there, on that soft day in June, I could see that it was a typical Ozark lake, with lots of trees, coves, and even a few low bluffs. It looked like it was full of bass and perch.

Jerry was anxious to get started. He rented a boat and motor and we both piled in, thinking no doubt of the many times Dad had done this for us.

"Got the flashlight?" I asked. Jerry didn't get it, or he was not being sentimental.

"Lake closes at sundown, so we have to be in by then," Jerry grinned. "Dad would hate that!" He apparently remembered after all. I noticed that it was about two o'clock.

Jerry twisted the throttle and the boat leaped ahead. I was leaning over the bow, feeling and smelling the spray. Suddenly, the stern of the boat rose and the motor shrieked with its prop out of the water. I looked back at Jerry and he smiled a crooked smile as the stern came down.

I wondered what he was up to. The boat continued to plow the water, then suddenly the stern came up again and the prop again ran wild. I turned around then. "Why is it doing that?" I yelled.

Jerry looked concerned, then kind of smiled. "I think you'd better move into the middle," he said. "Sorry, but there's too much weight up front."

I moved and the boat dug in, stuck its bow up and cruised normally. Jerry laughed and shrugged. I don't know how he did it, but somehow I know that he rigged that stunt to call attention to my weight. I let him get away with that one.

We picked up a few perch in a cove full of brush. Then we made a few satisfying casts in likely looking places but got no more strikes. Jerry kept looking at the perch on the stringer.

"Let's see, I got that one and you got this one and this one was mine, too." I began to realize that it was important to Jerry that he catch more fish than I did, and bigger ones, too.

Although the ambience of the fishing experience was truly relaxing and I didn't care if we caught any fish or not, I could tell that in Jerry's mind we were in a fierce contest. I also knew that if I was lucky enough to catch more fish, especially bass, Jerry would lose his good humor. Right then he was laughing a lot, mostly when he managed to make a better cast than I did.

We crossed the lake because the shore looked better over there. Jerry cut the motor and as the boat drifted he fevershly began casting. He gave the stopped motor some left rudder and landed his lure at the base of a stump. Immediately there was a huge splash and Jerry's rod bent double. "I got him, I got him!" he yelled. His face was contorted with something like fiendish joy as he whipped the rod and worked the reel.

It was a big one all right. He leaped out of the water, slashing its tail and wagging its massive head. It was a bass! Jerry had gone berserk, yelling about a net, which we didn't have. He kept his rod tip pointed down and worked to bring the fish in. Then all of a sudden his lure flew through the air over my head. The bass had gotten off! Jerry sat there with his mouth open, his eyes showing that he didn't understand why the lure was now on the other side of the boat. He worked the reel a bit to make sure that the line was not still attached to the fish. Then the reality sunk in and he threw the rod into the bottom of the boat. He threw up his hands and shook his head.

"It was a big one for sure," I said.

"I can't believe it," he moaned, "How could he get off?"

"Probably shook loose on that jump." I looked at him with sympathy. "But hey, he's still out there. Let's go get him."

"He's probably long gone." Jerry's shoulders slumped.

I had sat there through all of this and watched the drama without once trying to make a cast. Jerry had gotten all of the thrills and it was his tragedy that the fish was lost, not mine.

Before Jerry had fully recovered, I had my lure in the water. I was sure that there was another one there and I didn't feel any more sympathy for Jerry. I made three casts before Jerry reached for his rod. He was looking for another good place to cast, probably on the other side of the cove.

Meanwhile, I had a couple of strikes. "Hey, there he is!" I said. Jerry looked skeptical, but his eyes lit up. I was using a little red and white spoon and I threw it a couple of more times when, "wham! He tuk it!"

It was a good strike and must have been a fair fish, but not like Jerry's bass.

I fought the thing soundlessly until suddenly the fish gave a lunge for the bottom and bent my rod double! "Wow!" I said. "It must be a big one!" I began to feel the old thrill. Jerry just watched the rod bend. I began reeling, but the line wouldn't come in. The fish was pulling so hard that I couldn't turn the reel. It came in a little, then stopped. Jerry looked interested. "Wait a minute," I said. "What the hell?" The rod had gone straight again, but the reel still wouldn't turn. I looked closely and saw that the line was fouled around the reel handle. I cleared the line and began reeling in. I felt a jerk at the end of the line. "He's still on," I said. I began bringing him in. Meanwhile, Jerry was smiling again. The fish came up and I jerked him into the air. It was a six inch perch! Jerry laughed.

"For God's sake!" I said, disgusted.

"Good bait," Jerry said, his humor restored. "I guess that makes up for it." I knew he meant that my embarrassment made up for the ignominy of his losing the big bass.

Jerry secured his rod and pulled in the stringer of perch. Then I noticed a few rolls on the water near the shore. I started to make a cast. "Getting dark," Jerry said. "Best time for fishin' but we have to get back to the dock." He was brisk and grim, but still smiling. "I guess we don't get the big one today." He yanked the starter rope and the motor roared. I looked back at him and he was still smiling.

I knew it was because Jerry felt that he had bested me. He had gotten the biggest fish, even if he did lose it. And then, when it looked like I was going to get "the big one", it turned out that all I had caught was a minnow. Jerry would laugh about that afternoon for a long time. The joke was still on me.

########

CHAPTER TWENTY-FOUR

THE OLD TACKLE BOX

A fisherman will never throw away a lure. He figures he's lost enough of them to snags, stumps, trees and big fish. He wouldn't deliberately dispose of any lure unless he had to, even though that lure might be absolutely useless. Someday there will be a "fishing lure museum" and we will all have plenty to donate to it! Take a look in your own tackle box and you'll see what I mean. Except for that plastic bag of melted black worms, nothing gets thrown out.

If fishing has been in your family for years, then many of those useless lures probably go way back. Some of them might be antiques. I have one that's so old I keep it in my jewel box!

"Look here," Dad said. "This one was your Grandfather's."

It was a perfect little brown grasshopper and it looked hand made.

"Did Grandpa make that?" I asked.

"No. But it was hand made all right. In those days most specialty lures like this were made by hand. I don't know where he got it."

"It sure looks old," I turned the smooth brown bug over in my hand. The hook was not rusted.

"You know, it could have belonged to his Dad - your great grandfather!"

"No!" The occasion was the cleaning out of Grandfather's garage after his death. Dad didn't bother me with all the old tires, the '34 Hudson and a bunch of other stuff. I don't know who got it but Dad had a lot of help in the cleaning. I think they let Dad keep Grandpa's old tackle box.

"He used a cotton line with bamboo sticks for a stringer. And this old red and white plug must be fifty years old." Dad looked off into the distance but he was not ready to break down and weep in my presence.

"Let me tell you a story about this old red and white plunker," Dad said. That was the one which had belonged to his Dad. "It was when you were a baby, probably in 1928, and dad had gotten "permission" from Mom to take me on a little trip down to Tanneycomo. He owned a little strip of land on that lake then and we used it for camping.

"Usually we'd go to the main dock for a boat, then motor over to our campsite. This time we didn't get a motor since they were all out, so I got some exercise using the old oars.

"'Left oar, son,' Dad said, 'then pull for home.'

Dad was never shy about giving me directions."

"Sounds familiar," I said.

"Anyway," Dad continued, "The old man was rigging up a fancy new casting outfit. He had a new level-wind reel and a five foot steel rod with a cork handle. He tied an 8-pound gut leader about two feet long onto the black casting line.

Then he rummaged around in his tackle box and came up with this red-and-white plunker. 'This is for the big-uns', he said. Meanwhile, I had already rigged my fly rod and had tied on a black bug. We were ready.

"We went out in the boat and started fishing the brushy shore next to our camp. Dad was getting fair distance with his casting rod and I was whipping the air with my black bug. Alongside of one log I had a few strikes but they were too small for the bug. I didn't feel like there were any big ones around. Then it happened. Dad had heaved his plug up under an overhanging bush. He left it floating on the water and made the plug "nod" a few times. Then all hell broke lose! Like Dad used to say, "Kerip, he tuk it!"

"On your bug?" I asked.

"No, no, on my dad's plug! Something walloped it and took off. I'm sure it was a big bass. Dad was fighting it with his reel and making his usual noises: 'whup! Keep a-comin', woah! Woah!'

"Then the line broke. It flew back over Dad's head minus the plug. The leader was still on so it wasn't the knot. The bass had just busted the leader. About a hundred yards away there was a big splash as the bass tried to get rid of the treble hooks that still had him.

"If Dad was anything he was an optimist. 'Row on over there, son, and let's follow him.' I never argued with Dad. If he was wrong about something he usually found out soon enough without my telling him. It's true that I thought I was smarter than he but I never pushed it. I just smiled a lot.

'Dad-gum-it, he's around here somewhere,' Dad said.

"Probably down on the bottom by now, hiding under a rock with your plug in his mouth," I said.

"Well, to make a long story short, we went back to camp and had a great supper, then we stretched out under the stars and played 'Army.' You know, that's where one guy sleeps and the other keeps watch for four hours, then wakes the other one up for his turn on guard."

"Why did you have to do that?" I asked Dad.

"There were still bears around Taneycomo then and Dad had been surprised by one once. That's another story! So to put an end to this story, the next morning we were up at dawn getting ready for another fishing day. Dad had his pipe going and he had already finished one cup of coffee. I was still plenty sleepy and it was hardly light. I sat up on one elbow and wished that the coffee would come to me.

'I know, son, but you've got to come get it yourself', Dad said. About that time there was a terrific wallowing down in the cove by our boat. I thought an animal had fallen in. I leaped up. 'What the hell?' I said. Dad looked disgusted with me because I said 'hell', but he went with me down to the cove. No animal had made the noise.

We saw what it was. There, finning almost on the shore, was a big fish. He mouthed the surface and I could see that he had a bunch of treble hooks in him. In fact..."

"No, don't tell me..." I said.

"That's right...it was Dad's bass of the day before and he had brought Dad's red and white plunker back!"

"I can't believe that!" I protested.

"Well, there's the plug, right in your hand."

"So, O.K. - what did Grandpa do?"

"He said, 'My Lord! It's a miracle!' He reached down and pulled the fish in. That old bass was plumb wore out. Dad unhooked the plug with a minium of damage to the bass's mouth, looked once more at his prize, then let him go. I'll swear that Bass sort of looked up at dad as if to say, 'thanks, pal', then swam away."

"This same plug, huh?" I asked.

"Yeah. And that wasn't the last time he almost lost it. It was a hard-luck plug."

"Spare me another yarn like that," I snorted.

"I guess there are lot of stories about these old plugs," Dad said and got misty again.

Over the years I managed to acquire quite a collection of lures myself. I had the usual bobbers and plunkers and deep water wigglers. And I had some new ones that Dad and Grandpa didn't have because they didn't make them then. The whole line of Rebel lures and realistic soft plastic fishies for instance. They are irresistible to fishermen but I couldn't ever get fish to show much enthusiasm. The old lures still seem to be best.

"You see this old spinner?" Dad said. He dragged a out a black fly with a slightly rusty, silver colored spoon behind it. "This one is home-made. If the bass didn't want the fly, he was attracted by the spinner behind the fly. And if that didn't work, I'd put a piece of pork-rind on the hook. Caught a lot of bass with this. Dad always said it wouldn't work. He said bass are not dumb. I said I didn't think they were dumb either, just greedy and hostile. When they saw this coming at them it made them so mad they'd attack."

"Reminds me of the time…" I began.

"Oh no, you have a story, too?"

"I was fishing in a creek that was full of algae. The fish were feeding below the algae and I couldn't get to them. There were a few holes in the weeds, though, and in desperation I cast my black fly at those holes. I couldn't leave it down there very long for fear I would get tangled up. I was just pulling it up once when, BLAM! It was a good sized smallmouth and he took off with that fly to all points. I had myself a good fish but because of the weeds I couldn't land him."

"I suppose you're going to tell me he jumped out of the weeds and you caught him."

"No, he tangled me up completely. No amount of tugging would free the line, but I knew the fish was still there. So I just waited."

"What do you mean you waited?"

"There I sat on the bank of that creek with my line disappearing deep in the weeds. People came by and asked if I was catching any. No, I'd say, I'm just relaxing here waiting for a bite. They'd shake their heads figuring I was really dumb to have my line in all those weeds. But I knew that I had a fish on."

"So what'd you do?"

"I just waited. I knew the fish would move around when he got impatient and that eventually he would surface. Or I hoped that he would. I was ready to wait all day. Eventually, he started moving and I reeled in a little line each time. Then he came to the surface with his nose sticking out and I had him. I yanked him free and just as he hit the bank the fly came out of his mouth. It took me two hours to get him out of the weeds."

"Don't tell me," Dad said, "that's the fly."

"The very same," I laughed.

"All right," Dad said. "I guess I'll have to tell you another story about this old Red and White plunker."

"Another whopper, I suppose," I laughed.

"No, another story. You can believe it or not."

"About Grandpa?"

"It was in the '30's. I had talked your grandfather into fishing with me on the Eleven Point at Thomasville. "We didn't live there anymore but I loved the river and had many happy memories about it. I used to fish it on early dawns when there was fog hanging over the river. I used a fly rod and whipped bugs up into the riffles and let them float down. You know how I am with a fly rod. I'm a short range fisherman. No whipping out fifty feet of line for me. Just enough to get the bug where it should be to catch fish. And I caught 'em!"

"The purists would hate the way you fly fish," I said. "But I know what you mean. I can plunk a fly next to a log only five feet away and catch fish." I had learned my father's way of fly fishing, which might not have been pretty, but it caught fish.

"So anyway I took my Dad to Thomasville and he insisted on casting! No, I told him, these are fly fishing waters. Plugs would only get hung up on the rocks. But he found a big pool where he could stand on the rocks and cast down into it. He had seen the bass that I'd hauled out of there and he knew he could catch one with his big plug.

When he cast into the pool the current would take the floating plug down to the next riffle and he would slowly retreive it through the pool. The action looked good. The water was clear and not moving too fast. He cast the plug in a perfect spot, held it against the current, then brought it in. A red and white will zig and zag as it travels in. And on one of those zigs toward the opposite bank the pool exploded!

"'Kerip, he tuk it!' your Grandfather yelled. And he had it for sure. 'Hup! Hup!', he yelled and played the bass through the pool. But the bass was not ready to give up so fast. Suddenly he leapt out of the water and did a back flip. He shook the hooks free and at the same time managed to snap the plunker off Dad's line! Both the plug and the fish fell back in the cold water. Well, Grandpa's face fell. 'What the Dag Nab!' he said and raised the tip of his rod. But everything that had been connected to the rod was gone! I spotted the red and white being taken by the current toward the channel.

So Dad, he figured that if the river was going to take his fish back it wasn't going to get his plug! He dashed back to the bank and started following the plug. It got over the rocks and back into the river. I figured it was long gone.

By the time the plug had disappeared in the river, your Grandfather was in hot pursuit. He didn't know the river, though, and I heard him thrashing through thickets and splashing through ponds before he could get ahead of the plug. Eventually the time came when he was able to get ahead of the lure and cut it off from further adventures. He walked out into the cold, fast river and plucked it out of the water like he was a bass himself. When I got down river I saw him there, standing waist deep and holding the old red and white plug up in his hands. 'The Lord helps those who help themselves,' he quoted. 'So thank you Lord. I'll not be taking any more of your fish today, A-men!'

"And this is the very plug he chased down the river?" I said, holding up the battered red and white.

"The very plug," Dad said and this time he squeezed out a few tears for the memories he had conjured up.

Tackle boxes are more like museums than they are practical holders of necessary fishing gear. In fact, they're a lot like tool boxes. How many of you have ever thrown away a tool? I guess that's another story.

########

CHAPTER TWENTY-FIVE

THE LAST TRAIL

I forget when we went to Caddo Lake or why. But it must have been about 1958, after Dad had recovered from the nightmare of alcoholism and I had moved back to Dallas. As they say in A.A., Dad would always be an alcoholic, but he didn't drink any more. His personality had changed for the better. He was managing a half-way house for the Episcopal Diocese in Dallas. Once again he was working with drunks, just as he had 25 years before at the government camps. And once again, he was sober.

Jerry was an MD and had been "drafted" into the Air Force as a Captain in the Medical Department. But he didn't feel like a "Captain", he didn't like playing war and he didn't like the attitude of the Air Force, which he said was identical to that expressed in the movie, "Dr. Strangelove."

FISHING WITH DAD

Anyhow, Jerry wasn't with us. It was just Dad and me on a brief, one-on-one outing which, as it turned out, would be the last trail.

Dad drove his old brown Pontiac. Caddo Lake was almost due east of Dallas, on the Louisiana border just north of Shreveport. Half the lake was in Texas, half in Louisiana. But it didn't matter. I didn't have a fishing license for either state anyway.

There were a few rain showers along the way, but no "Texas-style" weather. I believe it was September or October. We were driving there for a week-end, just to wet a line and be together.

The Pontiac rolled down the two lane at 65, Dad's comfortable cruising speed. Dad loved that old Pontiac for more than one reason. In his bad days the car had been his escape. He was picked up in it more than once. In fact, I marveled that the car was still in one piece. Once he had driven it into a ditch and spent hours trying to get out, spinning the rear tires almost to tatters. The Texas Rangers had it pulled out and Dad was put away for the night. The first thing Dad said when he came out of the holding cell was, "You got a drink?"

Now I was in the same car with Dad at the wheel, soberly driving down the road to Caddo Lake. Suddenly, big drops of water began splattering the windshield. It was a "two inch rain", with the drops landing two inches apart. Then the whole road was obscured, as we drove through the leading edge of the shower.

"Aren't you going to use the wipers?" I asked.

"Why?", Dad answered. "I can see." Perhaps it was just an echo of Dad's former Mountain Man mentality. Or it could have been an echo of the days when Dad had had to turn the wipers by hand on his Model T Ford.

"Come on, Dad, wipers are electric now, you know."

"Oh, all right." He flipped the wipers on and they sludged across the window, smearing bug juice and clattering ineffectively. Obviously he needed new wipers. Now I really couldn't see anything. But Dad plowed ahead, delighted with the rain, thunder and lightning. I think he loved storms.

The rain had stopped by the time we got to the lake. The lodgings at Caddo were nicer than most fishing camps and would ordinarily have been rejected by Dad as too sissified. But by that time, Dad had become so civilized that he welcomed a soft bed, air conditioning and even TV. This was perfectly normal for the rest of us, but it was not like our Dad of old.

We spent some time at the desk discussing fishing licenses. I hoped that because it was the week-end nobody would notice. On the other hand they were using an air tracking system where they spotted fishermen on the big lake and reported them to the nearest game warden boats.

I don't know why I didn't buy a license, but I didn't. Even Dad didn't have a license for Louisiana, so we were supposed to stay on the Texas side. But who could tell? The border went right through the lake.

We sat in the bar for a while, drinking iced tea. I hadn't seen him do that since I was a kid. But Dad didn't seem uncomfortable or nervous. He had somehow gotten it all out of his system. He had found serenity. But when the waitress passed with a tray of drinks I saw his nose twitch.

"Come on, Dad," I said, "Let's go fishin'!"

"Want to get some supplies?" he asked.

"Like what?" I asked suspiciously.

"Tomato juice, bacon and eggs, bread, baloney, canned stew."

"And where do you plan to eat all this, out in the woods?" I asked.

"Nah, in the cabin of course. It has a stove."

It would have been perfectly normal to do that but for years Dad would have preferred squatting in the dirt, slopping grease around, squinting from the smoke. Maybe he would have done that if Jerry had been along, or maybe he had just gotten civilized.

"It's not that I've gotten civilized," he said, reading my thoughts. "It's just too much trouble anymore. I'll even let you cook." Then I knew that he had changed. It must have been part of his restoration process. He had learned not to care about certain things that used to feed his ego. He smiled his crooked smile. "We'll go camping if you want," he said.

"No, no!" I said. "The cabin's great. Jerry's not the only one who can cook, you know." "I'll go see about a boat," Dad said. The selection wasn't too good; two 12-footers with oars but no motors. Dad took one and said we'd just paddle around that day. We went to get our rods and tackle.

I am slightly unclear on what followed. The boat we were to use was tied up at a short pier and there was a boat launch ramp alongside. I remember Dad passed the ramp when he was walking to the pier. I was following Dad, but for some reason I stopped at the ramp. It was just an old fashioned wooden ramp but it looked peculiar. The water was green around it.

All I did was swish my foot on the ramp for a second to stir up the water. The next thing I knew, I was sliding down the ramp into the water. The ramp was covered with slick slime that just sucked me down and into the water. "Yeeoww!" I yelled.

"What the hell?" Dad asked, dropping his tackle and running back to where I was trying to cling to the shore with my fingernails. "How the hell did you get down there?" He grabbed my arm. I hadn't been there half an hour and already I felt like a dumb little kid again. All of my adult aplomb was gone.

"Didn't I teach you not to step on slick boat ramps?" Dad asked sarcastically.

"Just get me out of here," I sputtered. Dad laughed as he dragged me out of the water. I stood there dripping with my head hanging down and for some reason I thought of Jerry. He would have howled, thinking of the times I had accidentally soaked him.

I sloshed back to the cabin, changed my clothes and tried to dry out my wallet. Accidents like that rarely happened to me. Thirty years later I would do almost the identical thing at Bucks Lake in California. There I slid into almost a hundred feet of water trying to net a trout. My wife, Dorothea dragged me out of that one.

We shoved off from the pier and Dad took over the rowing. The lake was kind of muddy and looked like a bayou. Strange trees leaned over the water. Stumps appeared. It was mean looking water and I shivered.

"Planning to fall in again?" Dad asked.

"Yeah," I said. "If we get hung up on anything, I'm not going in to get it."

"Don't worry," he said, "there's probably nothing in here but gar, carp and catfish." Nevertheless, he brought us up to near shore and let her drift while he tried out his casting rod. Plunk! He put it right over a log. Wham! The lake exploded. Dad's rod bent and his face took on the universal look of an angler who knows he's got a fish on but isn't sure that he'll land it.

Teeth clenched, Dad kept his rod tip high. He was fighting a three pound fish which was on the other side of a log and was trying to swim under it.

The fish managed to do that, tying a neat half-hitch around the log as he did so. Then he must have spit out Dad's lure and gone on his way. But Dad didn't know that because the line was still tight! "What the hell," Dad said, yanking at the line. "It feels like I'm hung up."

"I'm not going in there!" I said.

"What happened to my fish?" Dad put his rod down and oared over to the stump. "Well, I'll be whanged," he said, "That fish tied my line around the stump and took off." He yanked at the line again. "And now I've got to cut the line to get my darn plug back."

It was refreshing somehow to watch Dad do something wrong. But we were a long way from my childhood, so I just shrugged.

"Take over the oars while I rig up again," Dad said. I moved back, took the oars and executed a perfect 90-degree turn, then did a few slow strokes to get us out in the middle. Dad didn't even notice how well I could row after 20 years of practice. He untangled his line and proceeded to tie his plug back on. He wouldn't use a snap swivel, and I just shook my head.

"Did I ever teach you how to make a knot that will never come loose?" Dad asked. "Don't need a snap swivel," he said, not looking at me.

"Sure helps change lures in a hurry," I said.

"Too many quick changes ruins your fishing. This old red-and-white catches a lot of fish without a swivel." By that time he was ready to cast again. We were closer to the other bank now and he heaved one that way. It looked like an impossible cast, but it went to a perfect spot. Dad looked bored. "I can put it just about anywhere I want," he said, reeling in. We were getting closer to the bank. He flipped a short one which landed just right. "No challenge," he said.

"Well, you ought to take up a spinning reel," I said. "I've been using one for years."

"Huh," he said. "That light weight stuff?"

"It can throw a plug farther than your old casting rod," I challenged. Dad grinned. Usually I would never challenge the master to anything. I felt a little heady at my reckless boast.

"Give me that black and white plug," I said, and adroitly snapped it to my line.

"That's a heavy plug for that pantywaist rig. If you throw it off, you have to go in for it."

Since the plug floated, I didn't worry much about that. "Ready?" I called. He nodded his head and watched balefully as his first born tried to outdo the old man. Actually, he didn't look like he cared much whether I beat him or not.

I rared back and flipped the lure with a heavy snap. The spinning reel did its job and the heavy plug flew through the air like a missile, heading for the opposite bank. I let the line go out as far as it could before I snapped the bail shut, and the whole thing landed in an overhanging tree on the opposite shore.

"Whoo-eee, what a cast!" Dad said.

"Oh, no!" I said miserably, and yanked on the line.

"You're right, son, I could never get that distance with this old line caster," he laughed. "I don't think I'd want to!"

I shook the line and twitched the plug. I teased it and yanked at it. I hauled and pulled. The boat started to move by itself. Dad grabbed the oars and started toward the tree. "I hope you can climb trees," he said, his eyes twinkling. "Maybe I can throw my plug at it and snag it. That's my good black and white, you know. You can't just cut the line."

By that time we were close to the tree. Fortunately, its branches hung low over the water and I saw that I could just reach up and pull the plug loose. "Here's your plug," I said. "Since I got more distance than you, I ought to win something."

Dad smiled. "How about if I cook dinner."

"You're on," I said, taking my rod apart. "I'll row back. At least we don't have any fish to clean."

The next day we had a few further adventures, including a scare when a game warden plane flew low over our boat. Dad caught a catfish and it stabbed him in the hand. In the old days he would have ignored it, but now he set up a howl and held his wounded hand like a normal person. We didn't catch many fish, but we had a good time, father and son, out of the jungles of adolescence and alcoholism.

Not long after that trip, I moved to California and Mom & Dad moved back to Missouri. In a year or so Dad had a series of strokes which incapacitated him. He never went fishing again.

########

CHAPTER TWENTY-SIX

HARD LUCK JOE

I watched Joe flip the lure expertly toward the fallen tree. The white and purple spinner-bug tapped the log and dropped convincingly in the water just like it had fallen off a limb. The bass thought so too, because he hit the bug almost before it got wet. **BLAM!**

Joe was not that excited because he was used to catching bass. What excited him was actually landing the bass and getting it on his stringer. Unfortunately this didn't happen very often.

Sure enough, after a hard fight and a few spectacular jumps the bass, about a three pounder, got off, leaving Joe's lure tattered and bent. Hard Luck Joe had done it again.

He was Hard Luck Joe, a spectacular guy, calm of demeanor and clear of eye. He spent lots of time sharpening his knife and thinking of life and the strife he had had. Hard Luck Joe, a guy without care,

<u>ready to go about anywhere. He took every precaution yet more less than often he'd pick up the prize. When he did, he was always surprised.</u>

Joe was a hard luck kid, too. He broke his jaw, broke his wrist and skinned himself up in all manner of scrapes. But Joe never blamed anybody but himself. He said nobody made him do all of that. He was just unlucky. But it was his fault in a way. See, Joe was so brilliant he was like a live wire without any insulation. He zapped whatever he touched. Geniuses always have a hard time growing up.

I think what made him the hard luck kid is that he didn't know that he was brilliant. He was soft-spoken and kind, affectionate and always smiling. He was a sucker for girls, yet he was not a macho ladies man. He had three brothers and it might be that Joe needed a girl like his soft and sweet mother to talk to without any competition. So that was part of it because some of Joe's girls threw him over. It was kind of like fishing. He'd be reeling one in and she'd get off the hook. Once he got a nice one on his stringer but she bent the anchor hook and got away with the whole stringer. That was Hard Luck Joe.

It was tough being in a boat with Joe. He had an uncanny ability to catch fish. Even though I would use the same lure and cast in the same spots, Joe would always pick up the fish. I know that I said Joe would seldom land the big ones, but that doesn't mean that he didn't catch a lot of fish. When the rest of us were being blanked, Joe would pick up hand sized crappie, bluegill and small bass.

"It's all in the wrist," he said as he flipped his lure into an impossible place. "Oh, blast!" The lure was hung up in a tree. Joe jerked the line and fought to get the lure back but the tree hung on. "We'll have to go in and get it if you don't mind."

"I thought you said you had to touch your cover, not get hung up."

"All good fishermen get hung up. If you don't get hung up once in a while you're not fishing in the right place or the right way."

WHANG! The lure came free of the tree and shot like a bullet back toward the boat. "I know," I said. "It's all in the wrist."

Joe was very familiar with most of the trees and rocks in the lake, having offered them his lures more than once. Joe was so used to getting hung up that sometimes if the plug was hanging free he would dangle it up and down on the water just to see what would happen.

One day he found out. Joe was using a purple spinnerbait and as usual he had cast over a tree limb so that the lure hung free over the water. He lowered the bait to the water once and **BLAM,** a bass up and struck it. So now Joe had a good sized bass yanking on his line, which was tied around the limb of a small tree. The bass was fighting the tree limb and Joe had no control. It was a spirited fight, but the tree limb lost and the bass got away. In all of the shaking the line came free of the tree and Joe got his lure back, minus the bass.

"Hard luck, Joe!" I said. "If you ask me I'm the one with hard luck, though. I can't even catch one with a regular cast and you're catching them in trees."

Joe caught another half-dozen crappie while I was reeling in sunfish and we called it a day.

"I know what you mean," Joe's brother Matt said. "He's hard to fish with because he pulls them in while all I do is draw a blank."

"It's the way he retrieves the lure," I said. "There's something in the action that tells the fish, 'that's Joe. Let's jump on the hook then get away!'"

"It's all..." Joe started.

"...in the wrist," we all said together.

Another time there were three of us in the boat and Joe was using a weirdly colored jointed Rapalla. Joe liked weird baits. If they had imposing or pretentious names he liked them even better. "Here comes Guido!" Joe would say. Then he had a "broken-back Rebel", a "Spitting Shad" a "Hawg Dawg" and an "Uncle Josh" frog pork rind. Anyway, Joe heaved his big Rapalla into the weeds under a tree. The bass, and it was a big one, attacked the Rapalla and got all hung up on the hooks. Joe was fighting hard and even his drag was zinging. The bass poked his nose up once and everybody saw what it was. Then Joe pulled in two pounds of moss.

The light on the water that day made little diamond flashes off the backs of the waves which you couldn't capture with your eyes because they moved too fast. That's when a video camera came in handy. The scene where Joe caught and lost his big bass was flashing with light and patterns like a cathedral where a thousand candles had been lit. It was a holy place but you couldn't see that with the naked eye.

Joe probably thought that since he always caught more fish than the rest of us the fact that he always lost the big ones was not important. But it was obvious to us that something strange was happening. Despite his prowess as a fisherman, he was Hard Luck Joe.

<u>Hard Luck Joe, always lost the big ones. Hard Luck Joe, never brought 'em home.</u> He sharpened his knife and thought about life.

The day had dawned in a spectacular fashion. Fog loomed over the quiet water of the lake. The wind was down and the sun was a pink glow behind the fog. The day before the lake had been a dirty gray rug running whitecaps and a lumpy sky was spitting rain. That's what made the morning so remarkable.

The dawn patrol returned empty handed although with some encouraging stories. At midday we made a more serious effort but even though Joe was in our boat I caught the only fish worth keeping.

That evening was the time of truth. It was still calm. Dave and I went out in one boat, Joe and Matt in another. The shoreline was one brushy cove after another and the water was perfect. But cast after satisfying cast brought no results. I did better in deep water with minnows. We were fishing ahead of Joe and Matt. Joe kept catching fish and throwing them back. I heard Matt complain that he hadn't had a strike. But David and I were in our own world, getting tangled in trees and bushes, catching the bottom, trying to coax the trolling motor to run on a dead battery. We were about ready to start back when the world turned upside down. A wild Rebel yell cut through the evening air.

We looked around and saw Joe standing in his boat, holding up a big dark object that I assumed was a fish. He held it up by his face to show us and the tail flapped on his knees. "It's a bass!" Joe yelled.

Hard Luck Joe had tied into the bass and fought him wordlessly for ten minutes while Matt looked on in fascination. But not until the giant bass was actually in the boat had Joe yelled. The jinx or whatever it was had ended. The bass was almost 24 inches and weighed over nine pounds! It was the kind of fish you have to use two arms to hold up for pictures. It was sort of unbelievable.

"What'd you get him on?" I asked.

"The Rapalla," Joe said. "But it was an accident."

"Joe," Matt said. "If you tell them what really happened you're going to ruin a great story."

"Why, what happened?" I asked.

But Joe had started his motor and was slewing the boat around for the run home. He smiled and waved.

Hard Luck Joe had caught the biggest bass, the most bass and the most fish. But then an odd thing happened.

After everybody had seen the giant bass and it had been weighed, measured and photographed, Joe let it go!

He looked deep into the bass's eyes and cradled him like a baby. The fish worked his gills trying to breathe. Joe must have thought about all the slaughter that was to come, the cutting and the hacking that would forever destroy the great fish's being. He thought about all of the other bass he would catch and eat but this one was special. Because of that bass, no longer would they call him Hard Luck Joe. He knew now what it was all about to land the big one. Joe lowered the bass into the water and splashed life back into the beautiful green and black body. The bass flipped his whale-like tail and sounded silently into the dark water. The giant was gone.

But Joe wasn't depressed. He knew he had caught and landed the big one and might even do it again. He knew that his hard luck was over and that the future would be bright and successful. And he knew that he had forever set the standard for his brothers' future catches. He was the one they had to look up to now.

But that night, in the dim glow of the cabin's light, Hard Luck Joe sat sharpening his knife, rubbing and rubbing and thinking about life.

########

CHAPTER TWENTY-SEVEN

SHOOTOUT AT PUTAH CREEK

When Jim Lehman and I took off for Lake Berryessa that summer week-end we had little idea of what we were going to do. All we knew was that the boat on top of the car was going into the water and that we were going to spend the night on a bank somewhere cleaning all the fish we were going to catch.

Jim and I had traded fish stories for years and I suspected that he was testing me. I was willing to be tested as long as I had a boat and a bedroll. I had brought along my old Pflueger spinning rod and reel, some reliable bass plugs, new spinners, a rusty stringer, a dull fishing knife, my Alcan Highway sleeping bag and a 22-caliber compressed air pistol.

The pellet gun would not kill anything but lizards and snakes, but it was good for target practice. Later I had reason to regret carrying such an ineffective weapon when faced with a jerk with a real gun.

Jim was a tall, lanky guy with size 14 feet and a size 12 smile. He liked adventure. He had read a lot of yarns and studied many expeditions. Jim was an explorer and pioneer at heart but he didn't get much chance to be either. He would probably have been at home with Fremont or Kit Carson.

On this day he was out to show me how many fish he could catch. But Jim was a troller, not a caster. He was more familiar with the High Sierra snow lakes where the popular way to fish was to troll deep with a Ford Fender; just run the boat up and down the lake, waiting for a big one to hit. My kind of Ozark fishing was different.

Jim was sure that my hillbilly style of fishing was easy and that he was just as good at bass casting as I was. Jim would have done well in the old days because he bragged a lot. He reminded me a lot of Mike Fink, the riverboat man, boasting and carrying on about how good he was at everything. Jim was very competitive and he would try anything once.

Jim knew all about boats and motors because he had spent many years trolling around big, empty lakes with no cover. It's true that he sometimes caught big fish, but the way he fished it was more like he just snagged them! Jim always passionately denied this.

Although he said he was going to show me how to catch fish, he was actually watching me to see how it was done. He would fake it as usual. Jim was a lovable guy but I knew that if he was lucky enough to catch only a few fish he would brag that he was an ace caster.

So we putted off up Putah Creek, which flows into Lake Berryessa. That time of the year Putah had a fair amount of water in it down by its mouth. The bass liked the cool holes and warm, rocky banks. There were rocks and fallen trees in the shallower water. Under ten feet of water there were ledges and shelves where the bass liked to fin and wait for minnows.

As we slipped by this ideal looking water I knew that it was probably home to more than bass. There were no doubt bluegill, crappie or catfish in there too. I was fairly certain that Jim didn't have much experience with those warm water fish. He didn't know what fighters they were or how good they were to eat, fried up crisp in cornmeal, their flaky flesh a delicate feast. Jim watched me with a curious look in his eyes, as if he knew what I was thinking but didn't understand it. Then he gestured with his free arm and said, "Does that look like home?"

At the end of a shallow cove there was a great slab of limestone, surrounded by small trees. Above it I could see a steep rise that went up about a hundred feet to the road.

"Looks good," I said, and Jim headed the boat that way.

We landed and Jim laid out a camp site. I immediately built a rock fireplace just like Dad would have done. He wouldn't have done it better if he had been there. If Dad had been there though, I probably wouldn't have done such a good job. Jim was impressed and put the cooking gear next to the fireplace.

We shoved off and started fishing. Jim had kept the big cooler in the boat and was consuming its contents on a regular basis. I pretty much kept up with him but soon I noticed that he snapped his fingers for another "fruit juice" when mine was only half finished. We fished along one shore and got a few small ones, but no bass. Jim wanted to troll out in the middle but I told him the water was too shallow. I showed him how to cast a plug right at the water's edge and bring it back with spectacular blops and splashes. "That's great", he said, "but where's the fish?"

"Jim, sometimes it's better to make good casts than it is to catch fish," I lectured. Jim just snorted. I could see that he thought Dad's philosophy about fishing was just a cop out. Jim continued to flail his rod and miss his spots. He caught no fish, either.

We were pretty close to the shore where some trees were overhanging the water. I made a couple of casts under the trees into some really great-looking water. Something rolled at my plug.

"Hello, there," I said. Jim was all attention when I made my second cast at about the same spot. We both held our breath as the plug lay there twitching and finally bubbled back.

"I'll get him," Jim said, and hurled his plug toward the tree. The lure landed about 40-feet up, in the branches of an old Liveoak. "Darn!", he said, and yanked at the line. The lure hung onto the branch for dear life. "Let's go in," I said and started paddling. Jim reeled in line and kept yanking. The tree shook like a bear was in it. I tied the boat and climbed out.

"What are you going to do, climb the tree?" Jim said. "Heck, I'll just break the line."

"I'll show you how to get that thing down," I said, and drew my pistol. The lure was clearly visible. If it wouldn't come down one way, maybe it would in another. I fired two or three shots from my semi-automatic. They zinged close and crunched through the leaves. Then I just let go at it, firing maybe ten shots in a close pattern. I could see the lure getting hit and bouncing around. Suddenly, Jim pulled it free.

"Well, I'll be danged!" he said, smiling. "If that don't beat all. You shot it right out of the tree!"

So I had, by accident I'm sure. Of course I took full credit for my eagle eye and uncanny accuracy.

Back on the creek, we headed for camp because it was getting late. On the way, Jim continued to slap water and curse his reel for snagging. Jim didn't have much finesse but he did have lots of spirit. We were right out in the middle and two hundred yards from any target. Jim had just fixed his reel and to test it he made a mighty cast to see how far the plug would go. And it just kept on going!

"What the heck?" Jim croaked. The lure never did hit the water, but Jim reeled back anyway. There was a tug on the line! "Dave, I've got something! But I can't see the lure!" Then, after a second or so, the lure hit the water. The line went limp.

"What happened?" I yelled. Just then a bat, or maybe it was a Swallow, swooped overhead snapping up insects. One of those birds must have grabbed Jim's lure in mid-air and had flown off with it. When it got a little prickly for him, the bird dropped it.

"You caught a bird," I laughed. "Or a bird caught you. Come on, let's get to camp."

That's all Jim could talk about as I built a fire and fried up our Spam and eggs. "By Golly, he shot that thing right out of the tree and then a bat tried to take off with it. That thing caught everything but fish!" I handed Jim a cup. "What's this?"

"It's the worst coffee you'll ever get. Drink up."

He did and said, "Glah! Mmmm, not bad!" I was never a good coffee maker.

The fact that I had built the fireplace, made the fire, cooked the food and cleaned the dishes didn't impress Jim much. But it impressed me! When I was a kid I couldn't do any of that. Dad and Jerry had showed me the way, though when we were together they considered me unable to boil water.

By supper's end, it was pitch dark. The night sounds and the water gurgling close by reminded me of other long ago camps. I peered into the darkness wondering if I would see Dad or Jerry in the shadows of the campfire.

Even though it was so dark I could not see the water, I got my rod and went down to the boat. I got in, climbed into the stern and flipped my lure as far as I could. I heard the plug hit the water and I jerked it around just for fun. Then, BLAM! There was a giant splash and I felt the line take off. It was a big fish! My rod bent double and I played him there in the dark without once seeing him. I was yelling at Jim, and he came down to see what was going on. Slowly I brought the fish in. He came up and I got him below the gills. It was about a four pound largemouth bass.

"I'll be darned," Jim said. "You just threw it out there in the dark and pulled back a giant fish."

"What can I say?" I smiled and got out my fishing knife. "Fish are where you find them."

Jim was convinced that all of my theories, skill and lectures didn't mean a thing. It was just luck.

"Just dumb luck," Jim mumbled.

"Not at all," I said. "It was pitch dark. The bass was probably under a rock out there. He heard a minnow in trouble splashing right above him. He thought he had a nice midnight snack."

Without another word, Jim got his rod and went down to the boat. He must have thrown casts out in the dark for twenty minutes without getting a strike.

Meanwhile, I cleaned the bass and cut his big head off with my rusty blade. I felt kind of sad and alone. Dad would not have approved of the way I cleaned my fish. Jerry would have derided my catch as being pure luck. Jim came dragging back shaking his head in wonderment at my wizardry. We both stared at the fire for a while then went to bed.

It had been a busy day and a surprising night. The next day we packed up and went home. Jim's fishing fever had gone down to normal and he didn't talk much on the way back. But I felt a sort of secret contentment. I had caught the only fish and Jim was reluctantly in awe of the "old master." Dad would have been proud.

########

CHAPTER TWENTY-EIGHT

GONE FISHIN'

When Dorothea and I went on fishing trips to our favorite lake in the High Sierra, the preparations were more challenging than the actual fishing. It would take us weeks to get ready. All closets had to be explored to find the proper clothing to wear in the woods and out on the lake. No matter how much gear we already had after years of fishing trips, major shopping expeditions were required to fill out our fishing wardrobes. Once I even got one of those fancy fishing vests with all of the pockets and zippers. I think I only wore it twice but it was a neat idea.

We had to make long lists of clothing and equipment. It was my job to review all of the pictures taken on previous trips to remind ourselves what clothing and equipment we had used before. Then after all of the details had been worked out the cutting-back would begin. Whatever we decided to take was always too much or useless.

I always took too many shirts and pants and not enough rugs, tables and lamps. I'll explain later. And whether the gear was lamps, rods or rugs, it all had to fit neatly into the back and the trunk of the car. The trunk lid had to close!

"Is everything we'll ever need in there?"

"Yes."

"What about..."

"Got that, too," I would say, turn the key and back out.

Everything would be fine until, after arriving at the lake, we discovered that we had not brought any fresh food. So the next two hours were traditionally spent at a local supermarket. The resulting grocery bags would be crammed into every spare space, including our laps. By the time we got to the lake the sun would be over the yard arm and it was time for a drink.

But the first thing we usually had to do when we finally arrived at the cabin was to chip out the ice-bound freezer which would lead to a complete cleaning of the refrigerator before we could even think about getting a drink.

We would spend the first day settling in and making lists of what we forgot and what we thought we absolutely had to get. There were things like rugs to cover the cold cabin floor, hooks because there was no closet, a fan because it might get hot, light bulbs because the cabin was only illuminated by one 25-watt globe and maybe a few more towels. Once we even had to buy a table!

The next day we would scout out our surroundings as if we hadn't been there every summer for seven years. But in the High Sierra conditions were different every year. The water in the lake might be extra low, or very high. One year there were six foot snow banks along the roads. We checked the weather for thunder storms and wind.

We hesitated to actually go out on the lake in a boat and fish. There was an unspoken reluctance to let go of civilization and give in to the camping mentality.

When I was a kid fishing with Dad and Jerry there was never any question that I would have to go out in the boat, lay on the ground, get scratched up in the bushes, get dirty, wet and fishy. At Boy Scout camp they warned us not to hang around the cabin. There was all sorts of pressure to get outside with a busy group and to forget personal comfort.

Dad reinforced this macho-military approach to outdoor life. Camping was only a necessity in order to survive. Camping was not supposed to be comfortable. The camp was only to provide life-support for the hero fisherman. The purpose of the expedition was to catch as many fish as possible by using a combination of native skill, fish-psychology and perseverance. No one who was a real fisherman and outdoorsman would ever consider just sitting around the camp, dozing in the sun, listening to the birds or appreciating the beauty of the woods and lake. That was sissy stuff.

But after I was on my own with no pressure from Dad or scoutmasters to do anything I didn't want to do I went fishing in my own way, which was as comfortably as possible. I never used a tent without a floor and I quit sleeping on the ground. Later I quit using a tent altogether and never went fishing unless I could sleep in a tight cabin with a comfortable bed and a good heater.

But when Monday morning came to our little cabin in the mountains I knew that we had to go fishing because that was why we were there. So I would drag down to the boat dock about 8 A.M., kicking rocks and looking suspiciously at the wind-ruffled water. It always looked cold and dangerous.

"Got a boat for me?" I asked the stringy-haired kid.

"How long you want it for?"

"Every day the rest of the week. I'm in cabin 2 up the hill."

"Take the aluminum boat. Got the best motor."

"Just put it on our bill. We'll be down in an hour."

"I'll gas it up and get you some seat pads."

We were in business. Half the battle of going fishing was arranging to rent a boat. After that it was just a matter of doing what I was trained to do.

Our equipment was pretty much the same as Dad's with a few exceptions. We didn't use a minnow bucket because live bait was not allowed on this lake. Dorothea discovered that back packs are good for carrying water, food and things like cameras and flashlights. When we were kids, back packs were not common equipment for some reason. Scouts used them, the army used them, but Dad did not. Some day I will remember what Dad had against back packs.

Then there were my tackle boxes. Though later I discovered that I could fish all week with a tackle box the size of a first aid kit, in those days I packed the largest tackle containers made. On this lake the only lure that would catch anything was a "Super Duper." Yet I insisted on bringing along all of my bass lures, the divers, frogs and all of the flies, poppers and other equipment from my childhood. The tackle boxes also held pliers, knives, scissors, knife sharpener, pork rind, fish oil lure, four different reels, extra line, sun screen, lubricant, hooks, bobbers and a first aid kit. I never needed any of those things, except perhaps the scissors and sun screen, but I always felt more secure having everything from the sporting goods store in the boat with me. With everything at my feet, including a big net and a 12 hook stringer, I would reach back, prime the motor and yank the cord.

The Evinrude belched to life in a cloud of smoke, then died. I made a slight adjustment to the choke and pulled the cord again. This time I managed to coax the motor to a regular sputter and put it in reverse.

Those are two things Dad didn't have on his outboard motor - an automatic reel return and a transmission. In Dad's day, when he managed to get the motor started, it just took off.

We sputtered away in a boil of wake, the bow of the boat rising and the rudder biting the water. A twist of my wrist and the motor climbed to its top speed, about 7 miles an hour. But it was enough to make me feel powerful. I aimed the bow at the opposite shore where the water was still dark and covered with mist. It looked like perfect casting water.

Years of experience with this particular inlet had taught me that even though it looked good and the fish were actually jumping out of the water nothing would ever strike whatever we threw at them. Still, it was so inviting that I could not resist starting there.

About 20 feet from the beautiful shore, I eased right rudder and killed the motor. The boat drifted and rocked quietly on the serene lake surface. The first try was with a fly rod. The fish were rolling at little beetles struggling on the surface. In but a moment I was whipping the air with my fly line, offering the fish my version of their beetles. The casting was great. My lure fell just where I intended it to. The water was like a pond and the mist added to the romantic aura of the place. But no fish ever struck my bugs. After ten minutes my arms would tire and cynicism would set in. Damn fish!

Meanwhile, Dorothea had been lofting spoons in long, perfect casts in quiet waters, patiently retrieving her lure till it clattered and dripped at the end of her rod.

"Why don't they strike?" she would ask. "Everything is perfect!"

"Why should they strike at a hook? It's so perfect, they can tell when something unnatural comes at them."

So then we would reel in and start the motor again, this time as quietly as possible. At trolling speed, spewing smoke, we would let our Super-Dupers out about 30 feet and begin fishing with grim resolve.

In about 15 minutes, if we were lucky, one of us would feel a tug at the end of our line. "I got one!" somebody would shout. That was the signal to kill the motor and whoever did not have the fish would leap for the net. A short struggle would reveal a silver-backed Coho salmon about 12 inches long which would end up tangled in the net.

It was always exciting to catch a Coho and slip it onto the stringer, but they were only about a foot long and they only struck when trolling.

There were exceptions. At times the water would look so good that it seemed a sacrilege to troll past it. So I would stop the motor, slew around and prepare to do a little casting at sunken trees and hidden boulders. Of course it was just a pleasant excercise, because no fish ever appeared.

Then BLAM he tuk it! It was Dorothea's lure and she was not expecting to hook a fish. However, she seemed to be a natural and horsed the fish to the surface where I netted it.

It was the largest spotted trout I had ever seen.

"It's a trout! A spotted trout!"

"Is that good?"

"You'll brag about it for years. And every time we come by this point, you'll want to stop and cast." I looked up and smiled. "Maybe he's got a brother!"

With that we both quickly threw a number of spoons and plugs into the area, but with no more strikes.

Fish are where you find them, of course, but in this lake the water looked so good that it was frustrating not to catch one at every cast. The fact is that good-looking water does not always produce fish, but bad water often does. We caught most of our fish in that lake off a rough, surf-pounded shore where we would spend hours trolling up and down, fighting the wind and waves and turning around every 20 minutes.

By the time the sun got low the lake was usually up to a wind-driven chop. Going home was often a rough and wet ride. Dorothea would hunker down in the bow while I navigated through the waves and took the spray. Eventually we would be behind the plunging breakwater into calmer water. The stringy-haired kid would be there to help us get the boat in. "Do any good?" he would ask.

"Naw, just a few," I would say, not wanting to reveal any success for fear others would follow where we had been. It was an old habit. I would always have mixed emotions trudging up the hill to our cabin. I missed Dad and Jerry but I looked forward to being alone with Dorothea sitting on our porch under the trees.

We spent many sunny hours with our chairs leaning against the side of the cabin, staring out over the lake, sipping cold ones, reading old papers and feeding the chipmunks.

We woke one morning with the wind blowing hard from the southwest and pushing the lake into the trees. We drank our morning coffee with the rain starting to spatter on our tin roof, then sweeping in sheets across the lake and starting a creek running outside our door. The wind rattled the windows and sent somebody's tin cans clattering down the rocky street. But we were in a warm cocoon, surrounded by the cold Sierra storm.

We had no phone, no radio, no TV and no newspapers. The little cabin we were in was at least 50 years old and had been used as a logger's cabin before there was a lake. Our cabin and all of the others in the camp were on skids so that they could be moved from one job to another. In the dim past this very cabin had stood in the tall forest sheltering lumbermen from the wind and rain. I noticed that the cabin never leaked.

In the bitter Sierra winters, six to twelve feet of snow would cover the camp, sealing all of the cabins in the cold darkness. I sometimes tried to imagine what it would be like sitting in there with ten feet of snow overhead. Up at the lodge a care taker would stay through the winter, keeping the building open and warm. We were never there in the winter so we could only imagine what it was like in that cold, frozen world. They said that the lake froze solid but the power company would continue to drain water out of the lake. This would result in the frozen surface of the lake sometimes lying thirty or forty feet above the actual water level of the lake. I could not imagine this condition and it was spooky to think about.

Sitting there in the rain and wind with the trees whipping around above us, I would often stare at the walls dreaming about what it was like at this spot in the months when we weren't there.

We got around to thinking about the Donner Party.

But there was always plenty in our larder and if that failed, there were plenty of fish in our freezer and the Lodge was well-stocked. Yet looking outside at the slashing rain and thinking of the frozen months ahead, it was easy to imagine those unfortunates who lay in their snowbound camps and had nothing to eat.

The few short months of summer made our lake seem like a fishing paradise. But the truth was that the lake and the camp were dark and dangerous places most of the year. As we left, driving down the twisting downgrade, images of "The Shining" and Donner Pass would come to mind. We were only adventurous when we were insulated from the harsh realities of the High Sierra.

When coming home from one of our fishing trips we always felt that we were lucky to have emerged unscathed from the wilderness. Six lane freeways held no fears for us and all of the urban terrors that the media mostly made up were our security.

And there was one other thing. When we would drive into the garage and open the trunk to unload, nobody would ever say, "Oh, I must have left it at the lake!" The only thing we ever left at the lake were brilliant memories.

#######

CHAPTER TWENTY-NINE

FISHING WITH A LICENSE

I've talked to a lot of Game Wardens but none of them ever asked to see my fishing license.

All they'd ever say was, "Howdy! Catchin' any? Well, good luck." For all they knew I didn't have a license. Sometimes I didn't.

Don't get me wrong. Most of the time I was properly licensed to fish but there were times when the document had expired. Let's face it - getting a fishing license can be a nuisance.

"Do you want a trout sticker? How about a lake trout sticker, a striped bass sticker or a sticker for steelheads?"

"What if I just want to fish for bass and bluegill?"

"Don't need these stickers, then."

"But what if I catch a trout by mistake?"

"Better get a trout sticker."

"How much is the license this year?"

"$40. Cash. Stickers extra. No checks, no plastic."

"How long is it good for?"

"December 31st."

"But it's already June."

"Do you want a license or not?"

You need a license for a lot of things in this world like hunting, driving, getting married, practicing medicine or law and to be a Notary Public. In most cases one has to pass some kind of test and demonstrate the necessary qualifications to deserve the license, plus pay a fee. But for a fishing license all you need is the fee.

You get a little pamphlet with your license that tells you all about the state fishing laws. They don't quiz you on these laws before you get your license. Anyone of the proper age can get a fishing license just by coming up with the cash. This is obviously a plot to raise money for the state.

The state Fish and Game people do good work and are partly supported by license fees. But that's not a license. That's just a tax. Why don't they just call it a "fishing tax?"

"Do you remember when we lived in Texas we had to pay a 'poll tax' before we could vote?"

"Yeah. It was two bucks. Lots of Southern states had poll taxes to keep the poor people, usually blacks, from voting."

"Doesn't that seem similar to the fees they make you pay to be allowed to fish? Keeps the poor people out."

"Yeah, but in coastal states anybody is allowed to fish the oceans for free."

"Big deal. But if you want to fish for marlin or swordfish or baracuda you have to have a special 'license.'"

"Got to have a big boat, too. No poor folks on big boats."

If you go out of your home state to fish you'll need an out of state permit. The fees for these permits are howlingly exorbitant.

"Nine bucks for three days."

"But I'm going to be here for 7 days."

"Ten days for $25. That's a bargain.

"What if I was going to be here for two weeks?"

"I can only sell you one permit at a time so you'll just have to come back for another one when that one expires."

"Or take my chances."

"Or take your chances. State fine is pretty high."

"How much for a bucket of grubs?"

"Dollar and a half. But I'll have to see your license…"

"Why don't they just make us buy a National Fishing License that's good in all states?"

"Maybe that's next. Then I could sell you stamps for particular kinds of local fish to stick on your National license. Good idea!"

I asked Dad once about fishing licenses. "How long have they had them?"

"Ever since I grew up, I guess," he said. "But not when I was a kid. I don't think my Dad had one. Even after it was a law he would go without one. He figured the woods and the lakes and the streams were his. He'd fished them all of his life without a license, why should he start paying someone for it?"

Fishing licenses were probably not common much before 1915, about the same time the Feds dreamed up the Income Tax. At least they didn't call it an "Income License."

The Game Warden's job is to see to it that all of the fish and game laws are enforced and that everyone using God's own facilities is licensed to do so.

Game Wardens are usually good guys with vast experience. The Warden is really the best person to talk to about where the fish are biting, what kind are being taken and what they're hitting on. And the Warden is sometimes a talkative type who likes to compare notes with you and give advice. But most fishermen are wary of the Warden's motives. After all, this friendly guy who knows so much about the woods and streams can easily deprive the fisherman of his catch, write him a ticket or even send him to jail. Who wants to mess with a guy like that?

I saw him coming up the lake. Somehow it looked like a Game Warden's boat. It was one guy in a clean boat with no tackle out. I'd better be careful. Just keep fishing and appear to be unconcerned. But of course I had to stop the boat and prepare to receive him. It would never do just to wave and then roar away. I assume that if you did that the Warden would chase you! That's what a cop on the road would do. Policemen make it known rather clearly when they want to talk to you by shining red and yellow lights and by making other unfriendly gestures.

In normal circumstances the Game Warden makes no threatening gestures or shines any lights. He just drifts up to your boat and says, "Howdy."

"Mornin'", I answer.

"How you doing?" the Warden asks.

"Not too good. Got a few Cohos." I volunteer the stringer to show him my fish. I figure that he'll ask me to show him anyhow.

"Not bad," he says. I am wondering if there is a limit on Cohos that I don't know about. The Warden writes something down. "What'd you get them on?"

"Super Duper. That's all they'll hit."

The Warden writes that down, too. Does he want this information for other people or is he checking on me?

"Well, good luck," the Warden waves and sheers off. He heads up the lake. He didn't even ask to see my license. I have no idea why he wanted to interrupt my fishing to talk to me. Wardens are funny.

One summer I was camped on a small California lake for about a week catching bass and bluegill. One day a Game Warden made a visit to the lake. He talked with everybody, looked around, checked the camp office, came around to me and said hello but, as usual, he never asked to see my license.

"Warden, I demand that you check to see if I have a current fishing license with the proper stamps!" I laughed at his expression. "Come on, man, I've been buying licenses for years and nobody ever asks to see them. Do your duty!"

"Well, sure." The warden looked at me like I was nuts. "Please remove your license and show it to me."

"Sure," fished it out of my pocket. "Am I legal?"

The Warden looked at my documents. "5-foot-8, 180 pounds, blue eyes. I guess that's you all right. You're all legal, sir. Have a nice camp."

"You're the first Game Warden who ever asked to see my license. Why is that?"

"I'd say it depends on the circumstances. You look like an honest fisherman who wouldn't think of being up here fishing without a license."

"You mean if I was a grubby-looking wino working a trot line at dawn or late at night you'd be faster to ask to see a license?"

"Probably, but you can't always tell by appearances. Lots of honest fishermen run trot lines."

"You know I've been up at this lake fishing without a license before," I admitted.

"Well then you're lucky. Don't do it again."

So I challenged the law and paraded my license before the Warden just asking for trouble. It was definitely my opinion at that time that Game Wardens didn't care if honest fishermen had a license or not. But if they encountered someone fishing in a "No Fishing" area or caught someone with more than their limit of certain fish or found undersize fish, then the first thing they would do is ask the miscreant to produce a current fishing license. The logic still escapes me. These persons had already broken the rules whether they had a current fishing license or not!

After a lifetime of buying fishing licenses, packing them on my hip and daring wardens to ask to see them I finally quit worrying about it. I still bought licenses every year and when I went out of state I still paid for three day temporaries but I quit keeping them handy and didn't wave them around.

One week in June, Dorothea and I were on a fishing trip at our favorite lake high in the Sierra. We had company that week-end.

"Hey, Dave," Dorothea's son John said, "You expect Toni and I to sleep in this rat's nest?" Our cabin was a little rough.

"Hey, John," his perky little wife, Antonella, said, "It's only for the week-end and besides it'll be fun."

"You take the bunk beds," I said, "and we'll pile up the luggage between us."

Having guests required me to get a boat a day or so earlier than usual. The kid with the stringy hair said, "Well, it's Sunday so you'll have to take the slow boat. All that's left. Tomorrow you can change boats."

The 5 horse Johnson would barely make headway against the wind and with four of us in the boat it was a slow go. I rounded the point to get out of the wind and we trolled on down to the end of the cove. "Hey," John said, "This is where we were last night on the shore where I fouled up Mom's reel."

"Right", I said sardonically. "Is it working all right today?"

John heaved his spoon out into deep water and reeled it back.

"Great," he said. I'm sure John didn't expect to catch any fish. It was hard enough to catch them when you were in the right place, and this arm of the lake was usually non-productive. But it was fun casting and retrieving the lures and sweating in the sun.

I started telling stories about Dorothea and I on this lake and what we had caught on it before. "They're out there," I said. "Your mother caught a huge spotted trout just off that point once."

"Then let's go up there," John said.

"Wait a minute," I said. "You know this is one of those days when the game wardens are out? But don't worry, I've never had a warden ever ask to see my license."

Then I saw the boat. Clean boat, single guy, no rods. Game warden for sure.

"Speak of the devil!" I said. "Where did he come from?" They all looked around and saw the boat moving slowly down the arm.

"He'll probably just want to know what we're catching," I said.

"Nothing!", John said. But he reeled in his lure and put the rod in the boat.

"Good morning!" called the boat.

"Howdy," I said. The Warden's boat stood off about 50 feet.

"Catching anything?" the Warden asked.

"Not a thing, Too many water skiers I guess."

"Do you have your fishing licenses?"

I liked to fell out of the boat. I was just telling them how in 30-years no warden had ever asked to see my license. And this clean little pip-squeek was actually going to do it!

"Sure do," I said, digging for my wallet.

"Well, I'll let you get back to it just as soon as you can show me current licenses."

I took mine out of my wallet and held it up. The boat came no closer. "That's fine, now how about you, Maam?" Dorothea was poking around in her back pack and finally came up with the license. She waved it. The warden could tell it was a current license by its color. "Now just show me two more and I'll let you go." I looked at John and felt a cold chill. John didn't have a license!"

"I left mine at the cabin," Toni shouted. She didn't have a license, either. They were only going to be here one day, why buy a license for one day?

I tried to slip John my license so that he could wave it at the warden, but the boat had come closer and the deception would have been noticed.

"I guess I'll have to check yours later, then," the warden said. "And you, sir?" he had come up to our boat by now and looked inquiringly at John. "Please show me a current fishing license."

"I wasn't fishing," John said.

"Would you please step into my boat, sir?" the warden said, coming alongside.

"Wait a minute, I don't need a license to just come along and watch do I?"

"I see four rods there. Please step aboard."

So John got into the Warden's boat and the Warden drew off a few yards. I'll be damned if he wasn't writing John a ticket! I had never seen this happen ever before in all my years as a fisherman. And it had to be happening to our son, John, at best an argumentative scofflaw. I saw John gesturing and remonstrating and pointing to us.

"What's he doing to him?" Dorothea asked in a worried voice.

"John's trying to argue his way out of it," I said. "It's ridiculous. John never goes fishing and for all I know he's never ever caught a fish! He's the last guy who should get a license."

The Warden's boat drew alongside again. John leaped aboard our boat, starting it rocking. He looked sick.

"All right, Maam," the Warden said to Toni, "I'll take your word for it that you've got a valid license at your cabin. The law says you should carry the license with you at all times." This guy was a real jerk. "The rest of you have a safe day and remember to always carry your licenses."

"Yeah, thanks a lot, warden!" I said. "I'm going to be here all week so I'll probably see you around. Don't get too close to my boat, though, it has a sharp bow!" I guess I looked plenty mad.

"Just doing my job, sir."

"Look, we're the fisherman here and as you can see we are properly licensed. These kids are just along for the ride today and I don't think it's fair for you to hassle them."

"Shouldn't be fishing if you don't have a license." The warden turned his bow and, revving up his motor, drew away at a leisurely speed.

"What'd he get you for?" I asked John.

"60-dollar fine!"

That kind of ruined the day so we went back in to the dock. "The world's only gung-ho game warden, here on this little lake. This has never happened before!"

I should have felt vindicated that a game warden had finally asked to see my license. That is what I had wanted all those years. Instead I felt that I had been violated.

DAVID LAMPTON MCKINSEY

I still don't understand fishing licenses!

#######

CHAPTER THIRTY

THE FLOAT TRIP

My brother Jerry should have written this chapter since he felt that floating reduced the stress of his tough medical career. He wrote about it once.

"From now on things will be different. The work will get no easier, but now I have a fantasy world to escape to when the going gets too tough. I have finally grabbed myself by the scruff of the neck and have fulfilled an ambition and a promise to myself made so long ago that I can't remember when it was - age 10 or 11 I think. I have bought a 19-foot Grumman canoe with a square stern and a three and a half horse motor to go with it. And now the rivers and streams of these beautiful hills are mine to explore and love. Oh joy, oh joy, I can't tell you what a thrill it is. A whole new world has opened up for me. Can you visualize the Current River, clear and cold and swift, most spring-fed of all streams, with the tall bluffs and towering sycamores and clean gravel bars? Down the rapids, around the bend, into a long deep pool along the base of an ancient bluff. There an old tree has fallen into the pool next to a boulder. There has to be a fish there. And WHAM the smallmouth takes the lure! Can you feel the strike? Outside your tent at night the whiporwills and the bullfrogs chorus. At dawn, in the morning mist, a bluebird lands a few feet away, unafraid. Montauk Spring, Round Spring, Alley Spring - magical names."

I wish Jerry had gone on but after that he was too busy with his canoe to write lyrically of what he was doing. These days float trips are a way of life in the Missouri Ozarks. Any tourist who doesn't take a float trip doesn't know what's fun.

The trick for a native is to find a section of river that isn't jammed with tourists because by now the purpose of the float trip has been lost in the rush to rent canoes to flat-landers and give them a thrill.

It hasn't been too long since that was not the case. Wild rivers like the Current, Eleven Point and White used to be almost deserted except for a few locals going from one place to another. Floating was not considered recreational 200 years ago when our ancestors rode keelboats down the Ohio and the Mississippi from Pittsburgh to New Orleans. And it was hardly any fun when Lewis and Clark took on the Snake and the Columbia while opening up the West.

At least one form of modern recreational floating was created by accident. Grandpa found that the best way to take me fishing was to put me in an inner tube and tie the tube with a rope to his belt. That way he could get some fishing done without worrying that I would end up floating down the river. It was a good idea which I didn't much care for since it restricted my movement. I had Dad's old short fly rod to fish with and not much line so all I could do was make short casts with my floating bug. I didn't have much hope of catching any fish. But Grandpa, in his chest-high waders and with a real fly rod, was able to hit the weeds on the bank and retrieve through the deep pools where the bass were. He caught three keepers in ten minutes. Instead of putting them on a stringer he used a creel designed for trout which hung from his neck and shoulder. Grandpa was having fun. He didn't have to worry about going further downstream where the water was deeper because I was safely floating in the tube behind him. I kept lashing the water without results but it kept me busy.

Then suddenly Grandpa found himself in shallowing water that was getting faster. I passed him in my tube as the current dragged me along. I waved and laughed but Grandpa wasn't too happy about the development. There was a rapid coming up and a slight fall before the next pool. He yanked on the rope to bring the tube back to him. But when he did that he lost his footing and splashed. So the tube proceeded toward the falls with me in it. That looked dangerous to me so I got out of the tube and started splashing toward shore. Meanwhile, Grandpa leaped up and threw himself on the tube to protect me. Before he discovered that I wasn't in the tube he had launched himself, tube and all, over the falls. There goes Grandpa! That's the way tubing could have started sixty years ago!

While Jerry found floating to be escapist and lyrical, I, the city boy, found it to be terrifying. To be a successful floater Jerry, and later his boys, had to have split second reactions and a certain attitude. This attitude was either, "what the hell you only live once" or, "I'm so good this river is not going to get me." I think that Jerry was above both attitudes. He became part of the river. I know that he taught himself to float and he never had a bad accident.

Floating down the James or the White is a far cry from the Snake and the Columbia, but the idea is the same. There's a challenge to keep the boat upright and avoid being speared and garotted by tree limbs and vines. The goal is the same - get through the rapids and over the falls without ripping up the boat, then float leisurely through the next pool, fishing as you go.

Equipment is the name of the floating game. Jerry had it all figured out. The lists that he made have come down through time and here they are!

<u>BOAT</u>: seat, cushions, anchor, rope, paddles, canoe clamps, motor, gas, waders.

Note the waders. Jerry had learned something about getting wet that he didn't pass on to us.

<u>CAMPING</u>: tent and waterproof, Coleman stove & lantern, white gas, bedroll & air mattress, thermos, ice chest, grill - charcoal, axe, tarp, food & equipment box, folding chairs, flashlight, air pump.

Note that Jerry, like Dad, still only carried one flashlight! But he had learned that sleeping on the ground was the pits and he used an air mattress.

<u>COOKING</u>: skillet, griddle, coffee pot, grill, utensils, bean pot - 2, dishes, cups, matches, condiments, napkins, detergent, scrub pad, paper towels, plastic garbage bags.

FISHING: rod & reel - 2, tackle box, license, net, new line & lures.

PERSONAL: money, cameras, tobacco, cleaner, extra pipe, matches, cigars, film, toothbrush, paste, soap, towel, wash rag, brush, mirror, nasal spray, prescription pills, Halls.

CLOTHES: pants, sox, shirt, shoes for car, underwear, boat shoes, gloves, coat, rain gear, sweater or sweatshirt.

These items were just for Jerry. Multiply that by two or three or four to get an idea of just what was necessary for an ordinary overnight float trip.

My first float trip with Jerry was a day trip down the James not far from Jerry's home. It was quite nice since the water was not too fast and the pools were loaded with spotted bass. It was a holiday week-end, though, and half the population was out on the river just to have fun. We floated past many a "tuber" out on the river splashing each other and cooling off. Further down river the crowds thinned out and soon both banks were just trees and bushes. It was an ideal spot until suddenly I heard twigs snapping along the shore. But they weren't twigs. They were bullets! Somebody along the shore and back in the trees was having a little fun and snapping .22's at us. That ended that idyllic day as we had no desire to be targets for some misguided hillbilly. Shades of "Deliverance!" Later I learned that the James float was only a rehearsal.

We had put in at Twin Bridges on the North Fork of the White River on a hot summer day. In Jerry's long canoe was our brother Mike in the bow, Jerry in the stern and me in the middle to provide ballast.

We rented a normal length canoe for Jerry's oldest boy, David, a white water freak, and Dorothea's son, Greg, a city boy like me. They were on their own. Each boat had an experienced white water pilot on board. As we shoved off I waved to Greg, who had never paddled a canoe in his life. I could see that Gregory was not sure about holding up his end. The two, David and Greg, were about the same age.

The White River at this point is not a wild river and Jerry knew it wasn't but I didn't. He was proud of his canoe and of his skill. On the other hand, he sort of had me at his mercy.

Jagged rocks lurched past in showers of spray. Turgid water sucked at unseen boulders and created whirlpools. The river was only about three feet deep which made it even more dangerous. Jerry stroked wildly. Mike dug in up front, trying to paddle away from the rocks. I hunched down in the middle with another paddle handy if, God forbid, my help was needed. Then the canoe crunched jaggedly on the bottom.

"Out! Out! Everybody out!" Jerry ordered. "Got to push her off."

It was considerably easier for us to get the boat afloat again after I heaved out of the midships and splashed into the river. The water was ice cold!

We came to an island, around both sides of which the river roared in restricted channels.

"Which one shall we take?" Jerry asked. How did I know? I was supposed to look at the channels, the rocks and the overhangs and judge which was best without seeing either end. Jerry had been down this river before but he had forgotten this little detail.

"Look," Mike said. "The kids are taking the left channel!"

"Oh, no," Jerry said. "I think that's the wrong one." He paddled frantically to get to the right channel.

The boat stood on one side, then the other. We were shooting the chute. But then Jerry saw why the channel he chose was not the right one! Bushes and trees almost covered the channel and sharp rocks stood in the middle almost blocking the flow!

As far as I could see there was no stopping or controlling the boat. It was going to go where the river threw it. I hunched down as Jerry yelled, "Watch the branch!" The branch missed Mike and hit me but it broke off before it could rip me out of the boat. Jerry took several punishing blows from the trees as the boat sawed through the rocks and was spit out the other end of the chute like a piece of flotsam.

We sort of went around in two circles until Jerry and Mike got control. Ahead of us David and Greg waved their paddles at us. "That was the wrong channel, Dad," David shouted.

"Tell us about it!" I yelled. I looked back to see if Jerry was all right and he was smiling.

"Are you O.K., Dave?" he asked. "Sorry about that."

"No problem," I said. "But let's not go back that way." Mike laughed.

I don't remember fishing on that trip at all. But we must have because I have pictures of Mike holding up some fish. Shortly after the chute we all went ashore for a little rest. The river was wide at this point and very shallow. It was plenty hot, too, but the water was cold. The next thing I know Jerry and Mike were taking off their clothes and lying flat in the river. David was doing the same thing, lying prone in the river, holding on to the bottom to keep from being swept down stream.

"Come on, Dave," Jerry shouted. "Best way to keep cool. But when I complied and assumed the position in the river I was paralyzed by the cold. The water was incredibly frigid, like it had drained out of an iceberg.

I shriveled up and turned blue. Gregory, the only sensible one among us, got into the river but didn't take his clothing off. He was soaked but later his clothes would stay cool. The rest of us staggered out of the river like zombies. Mike looked like the monster from the deep as he came out of the river with watercress in his mouth. Everyone was having a good time but I was a little apprehensive about more of those boulder clogged chutes coming up.

"The rest of the way is a piece of cake," Jerry said. "Only seven more miles to the take out point."

Float trips can be leisurely or hairy and I think we got the hairy one that time. Since then I have read a number of books on white water rafting, including "Running the Amazon" and I can see that in comparison Missouri float trips are pretty tame. They are relaxing like Jerry said.

And even though I opted to stick to lakes for fishing after that, Jerry's kids are all float fishing fools, taking a page from their Dad's book when he said, "Now the rivers and streams of these beautiful hills are mine to explore and love. Oh joy! Oh joy!"

#######

CHAPTER THIRTY-ONE

LAKE LODGE

I wrote a story once about a very old Civil War veteran who was being honored by young people. They looked upon him as a romantic relic of the past. He saw them only as an annoyance intruding on his memories.

It must have been somewhat like that when I took Dad back to the Lake of the Ozarks for one last look at the scenes of our youth. Dad was pretty disabled by then and I should have known better than to haul him around like a tourist.

At first he got a kick out of riding the road, going up and down the hills, glimpsing the lake. "Oh, boy," he would say over and over. But he might have been thinking, "the lakes and the hills and the trees and the old gravel roads are still here, but I am a wreck and can't enjoy them any more." I don't really know what he was thinking.

FISHING WITH DAD

I do know that when Dorothea and I took Mom and Dad on that trip down memory lane it was more fun for us than for them.

The folks had lived in Dallas for 25 years and had moved back to Springfield only a short while before. They had not been back to the Lake of the Ozarks for a long time. Now that Dad was back in Springfield he was within easy reach of his old haunts. But then all of his physical problems caught up with him and he was more or less trapped.

That's why I wanted to get him out that day, to show him the old sights and the old places he liked so much. It was supposed to be a sentimental journey. But like the old Civil War veteran, Dad didn't give much of a dam for sentiment.

In these leafy bowers we once hiked and halted to observe the lowly mushroom and listen for the redbird's song or the jay's loud cry. Further on we might unload our packs and clatter our cookware getting ready for a woodsy repast. Dad always said that greasy bacon and blackened eggs tasted like ambrosia in the woods. And after dinner we would hear the night calls of the little peepers, the Katydid and the tree toads. Close by might be a running stream gurgling over the rocks and singing its own song. Now those echoes were all gone.

The sign, old and weathered and crooked said, "Lake Lodge", pointing down a narrow gravel road. I almost missed it because the main road, though still unpaved, was a lot wider and faster than it used to be. Looking at the sign I wondered if it was the original, put up in 1937 when I was first there. I felt just a little like the twisty winding rocky road was leading us into the Twilight Zone. I was ready to go!

"Are you sure this is the place?" Dorothea asked.

"Says, 'Lake Lodge', doesn't it?"

"Looks deserted. And that sign wouldn't attract anyone. Looks like it's thirty years old."

About that time the road widened a little and there it was. Incredibly it looked just like it did in 1937! There were little wooden cabins with one door and tin roofs clustered under the trees close to the main lodge, which was a big dark green building with a rock chimney. The porch roof sagged slightly.

"I can't believe it, it looks just like it did, doesn't it Mother?"

"I don't remember," Mother said, "but it looks pretty old."

I pulled up under a tree. "Come on, Dad, let's go fishin'!"

Dad just grunted. I piled out of the car and ran down to the old dock. There were three green painted wooden boats. #1, #2, #3. I saw someone on the porch of the old lodge. I waved. I looked at the boats. They were banged up and old, with large rock anchors and tin cans for bailing. But they were dry.

"Howdy," I said to the old man who came down to the dock. He clutched an old briar pipe in his mouth.

"Want a boat?" he asked around his pipe.

"Oh no, not today I guess. Just looking at the old place. Brought my Dad." I waved toward the car. "He and Mom used to stay here back in the 30's when I was little."

"Oh?" said the old man.

"How long have you been here?"

"Just a year or so. Took it over after they cleaned the lake and they renovated this place."

"Renovated?" I laughed. "It looks just like it did in 1937!"

"Well, you don't think it would have stayed lookin' that way without a lot of work, do you? The lake was full of algae, dirty, gone to hell. This place was tumbled down shacks full of possums and pole cats. Huh."

"Well, I'll be…" I said. "Mind if I bring Mom and Dad down to look at the place?"

"Naw. They can stay in one of the cabins if they'd like."

The smell of a kerosine cook stove, rain pattering on the tin roof, the oily scent of an old 5-horse outboard, the thud of a wooden boat against a wooden dock; it was all overwhelming to me. I snapped my fingers and hurried back to the car.

"This is the place, folks, just like it was back in the '30's."

Dad looked around and snorted.

"The old man told me they had to clean up the lake and re-build this place. The lake was dirty and the lodge had fallen down. So they renovated it to look just like it did in 1937! It's incredible."

"That's nice, dear," Mother said.

"We can stay in one of the cabins, just like we used to. I'll bet there are a lot of bass around that point."

"Daddy doesn't want to stay."

"Well, at least get out and take a look at the old place."

"No," daddy grunted. He mumbled something else.

"What?" I asked.

"He says they didn't renovate me," mother interpreted.

I looked at Dorothea then kind of stared at the ground. I wasn't doing very well here. They didn't want to go back. Dad looked at me as if to say, "Can't you see I'm old and crippled and hopeless?"

I felt that Dad was sometimes too self-centered in his disabilities but that was a quirk of his. Sometimes he would reject the things he loved best unless he could get them on his own terms. And these days he didn't have much left to bargain with.

A cloud covered the sun and a breeze came up, ruffling the lake in a long moving wind line that swept by with a mournful whisper.

"I guess we'd better get going. This road is probably hell when it rains."

"Mmmm!" Dad said. For a moment his eyes sparkled. He was in there but he wouldn't come out. He remembered toiling up this hill in his '36 Chevy when the ruts were deep in mud. But that was then. Now the wind just rustled the trees and dropped a few leaves to remind us of the uncertain nature of the weather at the lake. I looked back once. The old man waved from the front porch of the lodge. In the shadow of the cloud Lake Lodge looked like a black and white post card, dated 1937.

#######

CHAPTER THIRTY-TWO

THE GREAT BLUE CAT

Jerry and I were never much for catfishing. We shared prejudices with other city folks toward this rugged fish which we thought of as "lurky" and uncompetitive. Jerry may have modified his attitude about catfish as he got more experienced but I didn't, until just recently.

I was back on the Lake of the Ozarks after 30 years, trying to get the smell and ambience of the old lake back in my nose. It was hard to capture the way it was when I was a kid. But the lake was different from those cold Sierra lakes in California and along with my visceral memories it made it seem like I had come home.

Dorothea and I were with Jerry's kids at Breezy Point Lodge on the Little Niangua arm of the lake. Jerry was gone and his kids were grown-up and we were fishing together as a group for the first time.

After a couple of days of great fishing, catching almost every kind of fish in the lake, including catfish, Jerry's boy David and I found ourselves alone in our boat, bobbing off of a bluff, minnow fishing.

There was an obvious storm coming down the lake from the west, but it didn't look too threatening and we decided to sit it out. Thunder rolled, lightning cracked. A gray curtain of rain that sounded like a waterfall moved down the lake toward us. We just hunkered down, tightened our hoods, closed our tackle boxes and waited. A few drops, then a deluge pounded down. Fortunately there was no wind. I kept an eye on our escape route in case it got rough. Rainwater was filling the boat and I had to bail as well as check my line.

Just before the storm hit, I had caught a hand-sized crappie and David had hauled in a scrappy silver (white) bass. With action like that, who cared about a little rain? I was getting soaked despite my "waterproof" jacket and hood.

Just then, David rared up and yanked his rod with both arms. "Holy cow!" he blared. He obviously had a good fish. His line was tight at an angle and began to run out. David pulled back on the rod and it bent double. The fish was still running and giving him a real tussle.

I was glad for him, but not quite as excited as he was. I had to keep bailing. As I watched, the fish broke water about 50 yards off the boat and jumped high in the air. It was a silver color and looked great.

"Must be a big silver," David croaked. I got the net ready.

But it took almost five minutes for David to coax his fish near enough to the boat for me to net him. Then he came into sight, looming up in the rain-splattered water, his big white head wagging from side to side, gills gasping. It was a giant white (blue) catfish!

===============

"The trouble with catfish is cleaning them," David said later.

"Well, hell, Dave," I said between bites. "You're the doctor. Didn't they teach you anything in surgery about cleaning catfish?"

Tim said, "That old lady showed us the cuts to make and how to peel off the skin. But we don't have the proper tools."

"Well," I said, "If we're going to catch any more giant Blue Cats like Dave's, we'd better get the right kind of pliers."

"He was 10 pounds, at least," Dave said, staring at the wall.

"Maybe 12," I said. "A great fish alright. Wish I had caught him. But listen, you guys. That's not the biggest cat ever caught, you know." David's head snapped around. "Not to depreciate your catch, but someone in our very own family has caught one bigger!"

"Come on," Tim said. "You?"

"Naw," I said. "Someone you know, though. Your Grandpa McKinsey! Not only that, but he caught it when he was a little kid. They said that the fish was actually bigger than he was!"

Outside the cabin, the rain had started again. This time there was quite a wind with it and a few lightning bolts thrown in. Thunder rumbled and the rain slashed the windows just as Joey and Mat came in.

"Boy that's some storm now," Joe said, shaking his coat and ripping off his hat.

"We had to stop cleaning fish because the barge was moving around too much." By that time it was cold and dark and wet out there but warm and cozy inside.

Finishing up the catfish and polishing off the Chardonnay, I pushed back my chair and smiled at them all. "You're a great bunch of fishermen, but hey, Granddad was the expert. But he got to be an expert only by making a lot of mistakes. He was a nervy kid. There's a story he told me once about a catfish."

"Oh, no," David said. "Not one of Granddad's stories!"

"Here it comes," Tim moaned. Outside the wind scraped tree limbs against the cabin. The kids were grumbling, but I could tell they were interested.

"Your Grandfather Mac," I started, "was about ten when he had a startling experience. But I'll let him tell us about it..."

=================

'At the time I was staying with some friends of my parents in their new cabin. Two couples they were and a sixth grade girl who used to make my life miserable, or so I thought then!

'The two men were fishermen and were always arguing about the best way to catch something. I followed them around a lot because I was interested in what they were doing. I was lucky they didn't throw me out. They let me help them with things and I guess they figured I was always hiding out from that 6th grader.

'About noon one day the two of them decided to set a trotline. You know what a trotline is? It's something like a bankline, but instead of having one hook a trotline can have as many as your ambition will let you. Tie a short line, a staging they call it, with a hook about every two feet until you get to the end of your line. That seems simple. But there's a lot of work to it. Keeping it baited is where it got its name. That is, it keeps you trotting to keep it baited. And any bait will do; chicken guts, blood meal, live minnies, even laundry soap. I've cut many a cake of Fels Naptha soap in my day!

'The spot they had picked was a little above a well called, "Sunken Forest" and the water was deep off the bluff. They tied one end to a snaggy tree and hung a yellow ribbon on the tree to identify their line. They let me row the boat for them as they attached the bait and paid out the line. When we got to the last staging they tied the end to a big rock they had brought along and chunked it in. Some modern trotlines are attached to floats, but this one wasn't.

'After we got back to the bank the easy part was done. The hard part was checking the line now and then -"running" it is called. And you had better run it about every two hours, especially in the night time. More about that later.

'By then it was about supper time and so the men decided to join the females and eat their skins full. Being as how I had helped them put out the line, I was invited to supper.

'After supper they jawed about running the dadgummed trotline but after a few drinks they decided to wait until morning! I couldn't stand this so I volunteered to go down and run the line myself. They looked at me strangely, but shrugged their shoulders and agreed. Go ahead, kid, they said to me. So I shot off into the night.

'First I got a coal oil lantern for light, then I ran down the hill to the boat. If there were any snakes in the path, I didn't notice them! I was on the dock, hastily untying the boat when I noticed how dark it was. I couldn't see anything; the other bank, the way the boat was headed or anything else. I managed as best I could and before long the bluff loomed up. The water at the base was very black and sprinkled with boulders. I admit I was a mite scared! Keeping my distance from the bluff as best I could, I coasted down the bluff looking for that yellow ribbon. I finally found it. Sometimes a bird will steal it if it isn't tied on good and tight.

'Well, sir, there I was in the bow of that confounded boat, bait bucket and light secured. The job turned out to be harder than I thought, what with picking up the line, holding that damn lantern between my knees and everything like that. But I inched my way along and pretty soon I noticed that the line was heavier than it was to begin with. Hot dog, I thought to myself. I think there's a fish on it! So I kept pulling on the line until it hung real heavy. I pulled the line up.

'But I wasn't prepared for the huge head that appeared from the water and I dropped the line! I had to go back to the bank to pick it up again!

'I can still see that head sticking up from that black water. Boy, that was a monstrous head! And the rest of the fish fit the size of that head. It was a cat alright and firmly hooked! It appeared to me it had been hooked for some time for it acted tired out. That was good for me because I was scared and had a fish too big to wrassle with.

'I realized I had a big problem which was how to get the thing into the boat! Various solutions went through my mind, including towing the fish behind the boat. I gave that one up for fear the fish would break loose.

'Finally, I just slipped my hand through his gill and out his mouth. I still get the shudders when ever I think about it. I managed to get to my knife with my other hand and cut the staging. Then I stood up and gave a big heave and over came that fish!

'Now I had an even worse problem. The giant catfish thrashed around, threatening both me and the boat. Finally, I managed to get him under the duckboards and propped my feet on top of him. This way both the fish and I returned to the dock, but to this day I don't know how because it was so dark and the lantern had gone out! But I guess I managed alright...'Once back on the dock I wasn't about to trust my fish to any live box, so I found a boat chain and ran it through his gill and out of his mouth, wrapping both ends around a pole on the dock. Then I padlocked the whole kit and kaboodle!

'I must have appeared crazy to the menfolk when I got back to the cabin. I was babbling about a monster fish, I was wet and dirty and actually shaking. They told me the fish would keep and that I had to get to bed. I guess that's what I did, but I don't think I slept much!

'Next morning I was the first one up and I couldn't wait for breakfast to go see that fish. Everybody else was kind of curious, too, so we all trooped down to the dock, me leading the parade. I looked first, with my fingers crossed, to see if the big fish was still there. It was! I was tickled pink at the uproar that the sight of that catfish caused.

'It was pronounced a "Flathead" catfish and it was promptly weighed on scales someone had brought. Then they stood it on end beside me. The giant Flathead weighed in at 50 pounds, give or take a few, and was as tall as I was!

'By that time several natives had assembled to see what all of the fuss was about. They saw alright and were impressed at the bigness of that cat that 'some little boy' had caught. Huh! Little boy, indeed. Right then I felt nine feet tall. I was mighty proud that day!'

I stopped reading Dad's story then and looked up. I think they were all with my Dad about then, seeing that monster Flathead being held up next to him, Dad grinning like an ape.

"So, anyway," Tim said, "He didn't really catch it with a rod and reel. He put out a hook and the catfish ran into it."

"Yeah, and it wasn't even his trotline," Matt said.

"That's true. But can you imagine how much courage it took to reach into the black waters of a deep lake, and pull up the head of a fifty pound catfish?"

"Fifty pounds!" David said. "Just think what that would feel like on the end of a spinning rod with 8 pound test line."

Outside the rain slashed and the wind blew. And I understood a little of where my Dad was coming from when he was trying to teach me to fish. Well, how about it?" I asked. "Shall we cut this cake now?"

It was my 64th birthday.

########

CHAPTER THIRTY-THREE

EASY FISHIN'

To most people going fishing is a relaxing recreation. In the vernacular, "gone fishin'" denotes a lazy day with no responsibilities. After all, to go fishing you just grab a pole and some bait and head for the water. Right?

"Professionals", those who go fishing a lot, make it seem easy. You see them out in their bass boats, practically lying down, controlling their steering remotely, lazily fingering their rods, glancing now and then at their beeping fish finders.

These guys seem to have it made. When they come in at night, their boats muttering up to the dock, they haul big stringers out of wet wells. They seem to have caught all of their fish with hardly any effort. And they are always neat, clean and well-organized.

But even though fishing seems relatively simple to most people it's still not easy for me. Going fishing for me is a huge undertaking filled with pitfalls and horrors. The idyllic pictures you see in sports magazines of two people happily flipping plugs from an aluminum boat and catching neat little fish which they put on shiny new stringers is all so much baloney. Let's face it, for a lot of us fishing is hard work!

It's 7 A.M. Do you see those two guys going out? Just to get to where they are has taken at least three hours of on-site effort, not to mention the 3 weeks it took them to get ready for the trip in the first place.

But to look at them you'd think they've been ready all night. Maybe they slept in their fishing vests.

The insidious, intense little sound drilling into your head is not a mosquito or a beetle, it's your electronic alarm clock. The hands say 4 A.M. In the books people roll promptly out of their sacks and wake up stretching. In reality nothing matters except another five minutes of sleep.

Who cares about the lake, the boat, the fish? It is pitch dark and raining out. It is a mighty effort to push back the covers and put your feet on the floor. It is absolutely miserable. The cabin is cold. There are sneaky little bugs everywhere so you shake out your robe and slippers. You need a flashlight to find the bathroom and your plan is to sleep as long as possible sitting on the can.

You light the stove to heat water for coffee and stub your toe on the table leg. There is no way you can get dressed and outfitted to meet your buddy in an hour. It seems hopeless. You sit limply at the table, sucking coffee and trying to keep your eyes open. Fortunately the morning routine is something your body will do without your brain. You can sleep while shaving.

By 5:30 you are close to putting on your clothes; jeans, denim shirt, boat shoes. But that's the easy part. Do you wear your watch or not? Find your fishing hat. Put your wallet in a plastic baggie so it won't get wet in the rain. Look at your wife still sleeping under the warm covers. Should you wake her up? Nah...

You are motivated to go through all of this in the hope that large fish will strike your lure and you will return to camp with a stringer full of trophies. You stare at the wall for a moment, imagining your triumphs. But it's sort of like dreaming about winning the lottery. It never happens.

Shove your hat in your back pocket and go out the door. Pick up your rod and tackle box and go down to the boat house. It's raining. So put your hat on and slog down to the boat. With any luck your partner will bring the stringer, the net and the minnow bucket. At least the boat is under a roof and is not full of water.

"What the hell, are we crazy?" I ask Tim.

"Got to get 'em early." Tim is fully outfitted in a yellow rain suit and is sickeningly enthusiastic. The only way I could talk him out of going fishing this morning would be to poke a hole in the boat.

I look out over the dark lake. It's only a light rain and there's little wind. By sunrise we'll probably be able to see fifty feet. So I fall into the boat and stash my equipment. As I sit there on the boat cushion I realize that I don't have anything to complain about. The kid is doing all the work. It pays to be older.

Tim backs the boat out, shoves it in gear and takes off. Immediately the rain hits us with the force of a shower head. The faster we go the harder the spray. I sit hunkered down looking at the bottom of the boat. But Tim has to look forward to try to see where we're going. I suppose to him this is a big adventure; the wild wind and all of that. I don't think even Dad would have been nuts enough to do this.

A mile down the lake and around the first point Tim throttled the motor down. The rain subsided to a steady drizzle. My lure was already over the side and I let out line so the spoon will flash over the shallow water of the point we just passed. But before the spoon got behind the boat a large silver shape rolled at it. It looked like a big smallmouth!.

It's one of those things that sticks in your memory. The bass had the spoon in his mouth, pulled on my line, then spit it out. Gone.

"Oh, no, it was a giant bass!" I moaned.

"What, where, when?" Tim muttered, starting the trolling motor. We swept back and forth over the point a few times but got no strikes. A "professional" would have swept the point and probably landed two bass!

Then he would have gone on to the next point, the windshield wipers working on his super boat.

"Professionals!" I mumbled.

"Huh?" Tim asked.

"Never mind, let's get into the cove and start fishing in our own bumbling way."

Tim pulled in three blue gill of fair size. We had agreed to keep everything unless we caught a bunch of big ones. At that moment "big ones" were as elusive as the sun. The drizzle turned into a steady rain. The boat actually needed bailing. My "waterproofs" were leaking down my legs.

"I got him!" Tim yelled.

"Oh, oh, hold on!" I got the net ready. Tim was fighting a shark or something. His rod jumped around, the line going this way and that. Somehow I could tell that it wasn't a conventional fish.

After five minutes of fighting, Tim brought the fish to the side of the boat where I netted it.

"It's a huge Buffalo," I said. It almost filled the net and looked prehistoric.

"Oh, no, I don't want it," Tim said.

"Well at least let's put him on that fancy scale you brought." Without undoing the monster I gaffed him on the hook of the scale and lifted him up. The needle of the scale creaked down to indicate 12-pounds.

"12 pounds!" Tim said. "Biggest one yet."

"So you don't want to take this monster back?"

"No way."

"This fine specimen of an Ozark White Perch?"

"Some perch." With that we unhooked the beast and rolled him out of the net. Not being particularly lively, the Buffalo lumbered away.

We drifted down the wooded, rocky shore, offering minnows and worms to the fish population. Not having a fish finder we had no way of knowing just what was there. But strikes here and there and an occasional Bluegill catch kept us interested. The rain continued to wear us down. Then the battery for the trolling motor failed.

We sat there hunched over our lines as the boat thudded into a log. I tied up to it because it was 20-feet out and sticking up from about 10 feet of water.

"Might as well work this cove before we go back," I said and let my line out to the bottom. That's when it happened. My line took off and whizzed off my reel!

I grabbed the reel handle and tried to control whatever it was that had my lure. "It's a monster fish!" I yelled, trying to stop the line.

"Probably another Buffalo. They're great fighters."

About that time the fish pirouetted out of the water in a mighty lunge. Water cascaded off of his silver sides as he plunged back in the lake.

"Oh, no! It's a giant..." **SNAP!**

The fish was gone. The 8-pound line was broken. I had never felt anything so energetic on my line. But my drag wasn't set right and I couldn't unwind the reel fast enough. I'll never know what it was.

"Excuses, excuses," Tim laughed. "But it sure was big and it didn't look like a Buffalo.

I reeled in my empty line. It fluttered forlornly at the end of my rod. It started raining harder.

We found out later that we were out about three hours, while the rest of our group had gone out an hour later and come in an hour sooner. They looked upon us as "fishing fools" and they laughed heartily at our tales of woe. I don't think they even believed that Tim had caught a 12-pound buffalo. Our puny stringer of pitiful bluegill was all we had to show for our morning of "easy fishing."

"So where's Dorothea?" I asked.

"Oh she went to town with Jackie about an hour ago."

"And I guess she left my key in your place?"

"Well I don't know…"

There I was, soaked to the bone, exhausted and discouraged, draining water from my pants with no way to get into our cabin to dry off.

A duplicate key didn't turn up for an hour while it rained even harder. I could only stand around under a porch roof while waiting for the management to try to get into our cabin. I finally decided to go to the boy's cabin, get out of my clothes and sit around in towels till Dorothea got back. Then miraculously the key arrived.

As I said, going fishing isn't as easy for me as it might be for you. I could have slept late, stayed inside and had bacon and eggs and hot coffee. It would have been the smart thing to do on a day like that.

But even though we didn't have any evidence, Tim and I have the memories of that wet and miserable morning during which we shared the hopes of all fishermen from the dawn of time - maybe it'll quit raining and maybe we'll land the big one.

#######

DAD'S

BENEDICTION

So, go your different ways, my sons,

With scalpel mike and easel.

But don't forget! On misty dawns

If you should hear a whistle:

One long, two short - it's not some

aort of train or Naval vessel.

It's me, your Dad, calling you lads

To come out to the bushes;

To fish once more along the shore

Of streams and lakes and rushes.

To be with me where company

Is something always mellow,

A hooty owl, a hound dog's howl,

A bull frog's throaty bellow.

Or would you rawtha, unlike your

Fawtha be modern, urban fellows?

So be it then with you, my lads,

It's like it's always been.

These longings always of our Dad's

To try to capture once again

Their scenes of youth, the glowing

Truth of comfort with their kin.

And so as your father, my father, h

His father each feeling lost in age,

Falls back onto wishing that he

could go fishing With sons who are

long past that stage, Until they have

    sons to whom they'll pass on

    The plea such as that on this page.

<u>THE END</u>

ABOUT THE AUTHOR

David L. McKinsey was born and raised in Missouri. He served in the U.S. Navy in WW2 and graduated from SMU in Dallas. He has been writing fiction since he was 20. He enjoyed it so much that he decided to become a commercial copywriter for radio and TV. He worked in seventeen different markets as a writer/producer for 30 years. *Fishing with Dad* is his first book.

Printed in the United States
925900003B